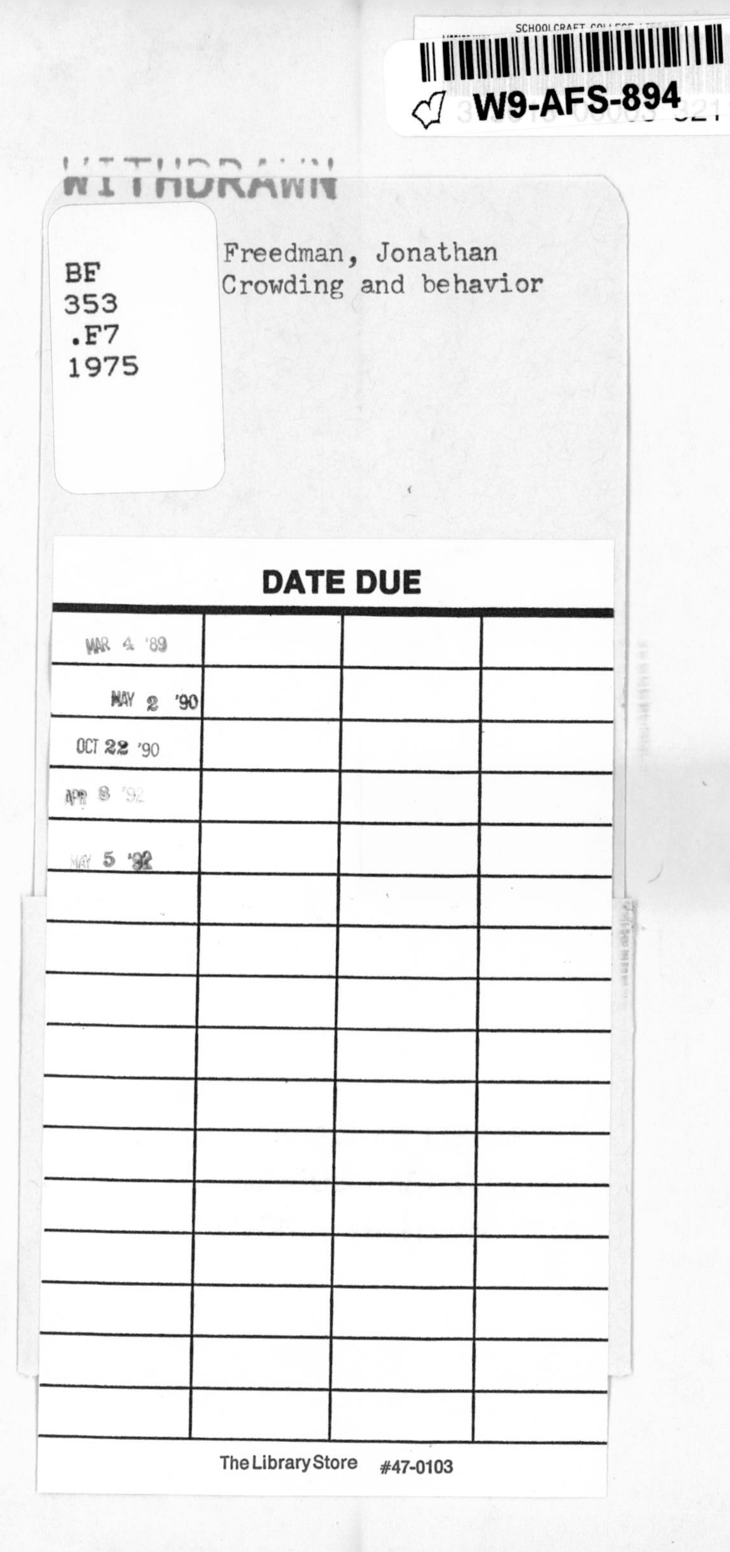

CROWDING AND BEHAVIOR

ALSO BY JONATHAN L. FREEDMAN

DEVIANCY
(with Anthony N. Doob)

SOCIAL PSYCHOLOGY
(with J. Merrill Carlsmith and David O. Sears)

JONATHAN L. FREEDMAN

and Behavior

The Viking Press  New York

First published in 1975 by The Viking Press, Inc.
625 Madison Avenue, New York, N.Y. 10022
Published simultaneously in Canada by
The Macmillan Company of Canada Limited

*The paperbound educational edition of this book
is published and distributed by
W. H. Freeman and Company, San Francisco, California.*

LIBRARY OF CONGRESS CATALOGING IN PUBLICATION DATA

Freedman, Jonathan L
Crowding and behavior.
Bibliography: p.
Includes index.
1. Environmental psychology. 2. Crowding stress.
3. Personal space. I. Title.
BF353.F7 155.9′2 74-6564
ISBN 0-670-24982-3

Printed in U.S.A.

PREFACE

How crowding affects people is a critical question for modern society, particularly for the great urban concentrations in which most of the population and problems are centered. This book presents an optimistic view of the issue, based on research over a period of five or six years by myself and a number of other investigators. We have concluded that crowding does not generally have negative effects on people and that, indeed, it can have either good or bad effects depending on the situation. This book presents the background for this conclusion, as well as its implications. Whenever possible, we have described the evidence in nontechnical terms, but more detailed reports of our own research are presented in appendixes for those who are interested.

All of my work has been done in collaboration with my students and colleagues at Stanford and Columbia universities. It is difficult to thank them all sufficiently. Paul Ehrlich first aroused my interest in these problems, Simon Klevansky, Michael Katz, Donald Kinder, and David Campisi worked on the research at Stanford; Roberta Welte Buchanan, Judy Price, Ilene Staff, and Morris Whitcup worked on it at Columbia. I owe very special thanks to my friends and colleagues Stanley Heshka, now at McMaster University, and Alan Levy, now at Duke University, with whom most of this work was done. Together we discussed, argued and fought about, and I think got to the heart of many of these issues. We do not all agree on some of the minor theoretical points, but it is fair to say that most of the research and conclusions reported in this book are a result of my collaboration with these two men, and I am extremely grateful to have had the opportunity of working with them. I am also grateful to the Ford Foundation and National Science Foundation for their generous support of the research and to the Canada Council, National Institute of Mental Health, and the Lehman program for providing fellowships to students working on this project.

CONTENTS

CROWDING AND BEHAVIOR

WHAT IS CROWDING?

Everyone knows that crowding is bad. Politicians, environmentalists, ethologists, and biologists constantly warn of the evils of high density living. They assert that crowding causes tension, anxiety, family troubles, divorce, aggressiveness, neurosis, schizophrenia, rape, murder, and even war. It is a wonder that the world survives at all given that so many people live under conditions of severe crowding. Yet live they do, and there are few reports of people in New York subways cars turning on each other in a violent frenzy or of shoppers in Macy's going berserk and tearing the merchandise and each other to shreds. How can this be if crowding is so bad?

The answer, according to research accumulated over the past few years, is that high population density has been much maligned, at least as it affects humans. Intuitions, speculations, political and philosophical theory appear to be wrong in this respect. Under some circumstances crowding may have disastrous effects on rats, mice, rabbits, and other animals, but crowding does not have generally negative effects on humans. People who live under crowded conditions do not suffer from being crowded. Other things being equal, they are no worse off than other people.

Given the degree of crowding in the world and in its troubled cities, this is an extremely important finding. If the world cannot conveniently blame its problems on overcrowding, it will be forced to look elsewhere for the causes. In addition, it will be possible to plan cities more rationally, using high density where appropriate and not using it elsewhere. The implications are broad, the ramifications significant. It took me and other psychologists working in this area many years to be convinced, but eventually the weight of the evidence overcame our doubts and preconceptions. This book will attempt to convince you also.

To give some feeling for the problem, it is important to consider what levels of density actually exist in the world. Although there are over 4 billion people on earth, the average population density is surprisingly low. If all the humans alive today were distributed evenly over the earth, there would be approximately sixty people per square mile. That means that every man, woman, and child would have almost ten acres of land for himself. Obviously no one except the most confirmed hermit or misanthrope would feel crowded under these conditions. Crowding is thus not a problem of numbers but of distribution—and, of course, people are not distributed evenly around the world. There are vast differences between and within countries that result in areas of extremely high density. North and South America, Australia, and Africa are sparsely populated; most of Asia (except for the Soviet Union) and all of Europe are densely populated. Japan, South Korea, Holland, and England are all more than a hundred times as densely populated as Canada, and more than ten times as densely populated as the United States. On the other hand, even those countries with the highest population densities still have a fair amount of space for each person. Holland, the most densely populated country in the world, has more than half an acre for every person. If the land were divided equally, every family of four would have at least two acres on which to establish itself—hardly an enormous area, but far from cramped.

Average density figures, however, are quite misleading. Just as population is not evenly distributed around the world, it is not evenly spaced within a country. People tend to concentrate in the more desirable areas, thus producing urban centers. Consider the situation in the United States, one of the least densely populated of the industrialized countries. Its 220 million people are spread over more than 3 million square miles (3.6 million if Alaska is counted) for an average density of sixty to seventy people per square mile. This means that there are more than ten acres for each person. What is more, the country is fortunate in having extremely fertile land, an abundance of water in most areas, and in general a higher percentage of usable land than most other countries. The intricate system of highways plus railroads and airlines provide relatively easy transportation to virtually all parts of the country. Yet, as is true in almost every area of the world, the population is highly concentrated.

There are vast areas where almost nobody lives. The Southwest and Alaska have very low population density, while the Northeast has relatively high density. And even within densely populated states, there are areas of low and others of high population density. In fact, most of the country has very few people living in it, while small sections around major cities contain by far the majority of the population. New York City and Los Angeles alone have almost 10 per cent of the people in the country, the ten largest metropolitan areas contain 25 per cent of the population, and over 70 per cent of the population lives in urban areas and their immediately surrounding suburbs. Thus, even in this vast country with its relatively small population, almost everyone lives under conditions of very high population density.

Cities themselves differ considerably in the amount of space available per person. Whereas rural areas might have ten people per square mile, even small towns have population densities in the hundreds. Suburban areas and larger cities have many hundred or several thousand per square mile. While big cities typically have population densities in the thousands, even they differ considerably. Dallas, Atlanta, Houston, and Los Angeles all have densities in the low thousands; Boston, Chicago, New York, and San Francisco have over ten thousand people per square mile. Although larger cities tend to have higher density, this is far from consistent. Houston and Los Angeles have very large populations and relatively low densities; Miami, Newark, San Francisco,

Boston, and Pittsburgh have smaller populations but much higher densities. And of course within the cities there are major differences in density from one part to another. The prototypical example is New York City, which has quite low density on Staten Island, somewhat higher in Queens and the Bronx, even higher in Brooklyn, and a whopping seventy thousand people per square mile on Manhattan Island.

These density figures for cities and parts of cities give an idea of the tremendous concentration of people that exists in the United States today. It might still be asked, Just how crowded do people find themselves in their day-to-day lives? They are surrounded by fifty thousand or two hundred thousand other people, but as they pursue their daily activities how much actual space do they have available to them? As a baseline, consider that the standard amount of space that is supposed to be available in American prison cells is 38.5 square feet per person. This obviously is not meant to be spacious quarters, but the minimum amount of space that would be considered humane and healthy. Jails in Washington, D.C., actually have only about nineteen square feet per person, Pullman cars (if anyone can remember what they were) and World War II troop ships both had ten square feet per person. In contrast, a typical nightclub has ten square feet and a theater seven square feet, comparable to the amount of living space available in a nineteenth-century London slum, which is estimated at nine square feet per person. At the bottom of the list, the Nazi concentration camp at Belsen had three square feet per person, while tied for last place, with about two square feet per person, are the Black Hole of Calcutta and the New York subway at rush hour.

Now of course these various conditions differ enormously in ways other than density—for example, in the amount of heat, odor, air, and cleanliness; in whether or not the individual needs to move around; in whether or not the individual is present voluntarily; and, perhaps most important, in the length of time spent under these conditions, varying from a few moments to a lifetime. The main point of this list is to show that for relatively brief periods individuals are exposed to conditions of extremely high density—sometimes, as in the case of a subway car, combined with severe unpleasantness due to other factors.

It is important to realize that the existence of high concentrations of human beings is not a new phenomenon in the history of the world. There is evidence that from the beginning of his history man tended to live under conditions of high density. Neanderthal man did not live a solitary existence, nor did he live in groups of two or three. Rather, he banded together in fairly large groups for purposes of protection, hunting, and perhaps sociability. This was even more true of Cro-Magnon man. Archaeologists have discovered Cro-Magnon caves in which sixty or more men lived. The population density of these caves probably exceeded that of any modern dwelling, and perhaps even the density per acre of modern cities. Neanderthal man, Cro-Magnon man, and from his first appearance on earth, *Homo sapiens* lived in high concentrations.

There are obviously many reasons why primitive man had to group together. One function of the group was protection from predators. Bengal tigers and other fierce beasts might occasionally attack a human being, and a group of men were more likely to be able to defend themselves than the isolated individual. Although this is an obvious reason, it may tend to be exaggerated by some ethologists. Man is not as big or strong or fast as some of the predators, but he is far from the helpless creature that he is sometimes made out to be. At five feet and about 150 pounds, he was bigger than most of the other animals around. In addition, although he is not as fast as many animals and particularly in a short space cannot attain very high speeds, he has tremendous endurance and can outrun practically any other animal over distances of several miles. A faster animal that could get close enough might be able to catch him, but given even a reasonable lead a man could stay away from virtually any predator. Physically, *Homo sapiens* is no weakling—and the early specimens did not have desk jobs. A healthy, muscular man who lives outside and gets a lot of exercise is an animal to reckon with.

With his long arms, a man armed even with just a rock or stick would be a fierce antagonist, able to put up a fight against all but the largest jungle creatures. Thus, although there is no question but that a band of men offered more protection than a smaller group, it seems unlikely that man would have to live in groups larger than two or three adult males simply for purposes of defending himself against predators.

A second, and probably more compelling reason, was to assist each other in hunting. Studies of primitive tribes in Australia and Africa indicate that a group of determined men can bring down animals even as large as a giraffe. To do this, however, requires a fairly large hunting party which chases the animal and also has the strength to bring the dead carcass back to the settlement. If the hunting party has eight men in it, the total settlement must number at least twelve adult males, plus females and children. Thus, for purposes of hunting big game, a colony of approximately forty would be close to a minimum. Therefore, to the extent that early man depended on killing large animals for his sustenance he had to live in quite large groups.

Protection and hunting may be sufficient reasons for man to live together. It has been suggested that there may also be a strong tendency toward gregariousness built into man's genetic makeup. Those men who lived together would tend to survive better than those who tended to be solitary. In addition, those men who *liked* living together would probably function better in the small societies that existed. For both reasons, a tendency to be gregarious would have high survival value, and by a simple Darwinian process more and more men would have that tendency. Whether or not this genetic speculation is correct, it is unquestionable that man is a highly gregarious animal and probably always has been.

Accordingly, it seems odd to argue that living under conditions of high population density would have bad effects on human beings. Rather than requiring a great deal of space around him. man seems to like living in close contact with his own kind. Naturally, under some circumstances a man might defend a particular cave or defend his family or country, but this would be for reasons of economic or physical necessity rather than from an instinctive urge to keep other human beings away.

The fact that man has always lived under conditions of high density makes the modern city seem less strange and unnatural than some people would have us believe. Instead of being an aberration or discontinuity in the history of man, the city has always existed; it is simply larger now than it has been before. It is not necessarily more densely populated, nor does it have different functions from what it used to have. The major change is that there are more cities, they are larger, and the social structure in the world is more complex than it was in primitive times. It would be a mistake to think that the "natural" state of man is to live by himself in the wilderness. Man has almost never lived by himself. If it makes any sense at all to talk about what is natural in man's heritage, the "natural" tendency appears to be to live in fairly large groups, in quite high concentrations, under fairly high population density.

Knowing that man has lived under conditions of high density for thousands of years puts the plight of the city in an entirely different context. It makes it much *less* likely that there are psychological or instinctive negative reactions to high density and increases the likelihood that whatever problems the cities have are due to factors other than high population density. Furthermore, it raises the possibility that high density, rather than being negative, might be a natural state for humans and may accordingly have positive effects under some circumstances.

Indeed the research on which this book is based has produced two major findings. First, high density (crowding) does not have generally negative effects on humans. Overall, with other factors equated, living, working, or spending time for any reason under conditions of high density does not harm people. It does not produce any kind of physical, mental, or social pathology. People who experience high density are just as healthy, happy, and productive as those who experience lower density.

Second, high density does have effects on people, but

these effects depend on other factors in the situation. Under some circumstances high density makes people more competitive and aggressive, but under others it has the opposite effect. High density can cause people to be friendlier and also less friendly. And under certain conditions, the reactions are different for men and women. This book will present a theory of density that attempts to explain all of these diverse effects. For the moment, the important point is that density does have important predictable consequences which are neither always negative nor always positive.

The two major findings are thus closely related—crowding is not generally bad, and its effect depends on the particular set of circumstances.

Before trying to answer in detail the question of how crowding affects human beings, it is obviously crucial to understand just what is meant by *crowded.* The problem is not just one of definition but of conceptualization. All too often, serious writers on crowding have become hopelessly confused because everyone is talking about something different. There are several aspects to the question, and it is important to spell them out in detail.

Ordinarily the idea of being crowded suggests a subway train during rush hour, the exit ramp from the second level of a football stadium, the bargain basement at Filene's or Macy's on a Saturday afternoon, or a packed elevator in an office building. It might also suggest nine people crowded into a Ford Falcon, twenty-eight people in one telephone booth, or even the special exhibit hall in the Museum of Modern Art during a particularly popular show. All these situations would probably be considered crowded by most of the people that participated in them, even though some of the incidents are obviously much less pleasant than others.

These typical examples of crowding differ from each other in many ways. Some involve great numbers of people; others involve relatively few. Some involve a great deal of activity; others involve relatively little. In some, all the people know each other and in others they don't. And so on. The problem is to abstract from these situations the crucial element or elements that cause them to be considered crowded and distinguish them from factors that are extraneous to the condition of being crowded.

Although there has been considerable disagreement on this point, it seems clear that the one critical element in any crowded situation is that there is not very much space relative to the number of people. The size of the room by itself is not critical. A tiny room can be uncrowded and a huge stadium crowded, depending on the number of people present. Of course, it will take more people to make a stadium crowded than it will to make a tiny room crowded, but the necessary condition for crowding is that there be little space per person. Similarly, there is a tendency to associate heat and odor and discomfort with being crowded, but none of these elements is absolutely crucial. The four hundred riders packed into a subway car during rush hour are crowded whether or not the car is air-conditioned. If the air conditioning keeps the car cool, they will be less uncomfortable—but no less crowded. The people streaming out of the football stadium along the narrow corridors are closely bunched together and ordinarily will experience the strong odors arising from the mass of other people. But even if they were all freshly showered and virtually odorless, the teeming mass would still be crowded together. A theater lobby during intermission is often cool (because it is well air-conditioned) and relatively odorless (except for the cigarette smoke), and it may not even be physically uncomfortable—but if there are sufficient people in the lobby, it will be very crowded. It is apparent that the one element necessary to produce crowding is, plain and simple, the amount of space available per person. The less space per person, the more crowded the situation. This factor, which can be called the population density or simply density, is the basic element that determines whether or not a situation is crowded.

If crowding is conceived in purely physical terms, lack of space is the only crucial element; however, crowding may also be conceptualized as an internal state. People "feel" crowded. The sensation of being crowded, of experiencing crowding, is related to but distinct from the physical state of having little space. There are times when there is very little space but the individual does not feel crowded; there are other times when there is a lot more space but the person does feel crowded. Some lovely summer day you decide you want to go off by yourself and be alone. You drive for an hour or two, hike through the woods, and come to a lovely clearing where you can sit next to a waterfall and enjoy solitude and beauty. As you enter the clearing you discover that at one side an enormous tent has been erected and a dozen people are sitting near it having a picnic. At the other side of the clearing four or five couples have laid out sleeping bags and are camped for the day. Although there is still an enormous amount of space per person, you may experience a feeling which you would call being crowded. Or imagine driving out to your favorite beach and finding that ten thousand other people have the same idea. There is still plenty of space for you to put down your towels and be five or ten feet away from the closest people, but you may say that the beach is very crowded and experience that sensation yourself. What is the relationship between these sensations of crowding and the physical state of having very little space?

It must be kept in mind that the sensation of being crowded does not always follow from or coincide with the physical situation. The *physical* state has no inherent value one way or the other. It is neither good nor bad by itself. In contrast, the *sensation* of being crowded is almost by definition a negative one. People do not say "I feel crowded, isn't that nice." "Three's a crowd" is not meant invitingly. Whenever a person experiences a sensation of being crowded, he is saying he does not like a situation he is in. When people have very little space but do not experience crowding, or are not aware of feeling crowded, then they are not finding the situation negative; whenever people do feel crowded, they are.

In other words, the term *crowding* has negative connotations; the physical state of having little space is not necessarily negative. Much of the confusion in writing about this problem has arisen because some authors are referring to the physical state and others are referring to the internal feeling. Since the sensation of being crowded is always negative, it would be senseless to talk about that kind of "crowding" as having good effects or not having bad effects. On the other hand, the physical state is neutral, and most of the research indicates that it does not necessarily have negative effects. Authors who use the term one way are sometimes flabbergasted by the comments of authors who are using the term the other way. The premise of this book, which is that crowding is not necessarily negative, refers of course to the physical state of not having much space—not to the internal state. The term *crowding* should be understood always as referring to the physical situation of high density, not to an internal feeling. The question under discussion is how a person is affected by that physical situation, how high density affects the behavior, feelings, and health of people.

2 COLONIES, SWARMS, AND HERDS

In exploring the effects of crowding on humans, a natural starting place is to see what it does to other animals. For many years the scientific research on crowding involved only nonhumans, and it is this research that is generally quoted in articles on the effects of crowding. Although some of this research is rather sloppy by modern standards or is based on rough observations, there is little question but that dramatic reactions sometimes occur when animals are very crowded.

Most people have probably heard of the suicidal march of the lemmings to the sea. These rodents, which are essentially mice with fur, live on the cold, inhospitable tundra of Norway. Their population undergoes drastic fluctuations. The colonies grow and grow until there are huge numbers of lemmings roaming about. At some point they begin to wander far from their usual habitat, and at the same time their population begins to drop sharply. Their wild, frantic wanderings eventually take them to cliffs overlooking the sea. It seems to witnesses that they deliberately head for these cliffs and that, presumably in a state of severe depression or because of some internal, instinctive urge toward self-destruction, they throw themselves into the water and are drowned. Since the fight for survival is such a strong impulse in all animals, this apparent suicide has been considered an almost unique phenomenon, caused by the extreme overcrowding of the lemming population.

This is touching and romantic, but the true story is less baffling and unusual (though no less fatal for the lemmings). What actually occurs is that the lemming population increases as long as there is sufficient food. When the population reaches a certain size, it becomes too great for the amount of vegetation in the normal grazing area. This results in the stripping of the land, making matters even worse. Instead of the vegetation being able to replace itself as it usually does, it is eaten so clean that no new growth appears until it has some time to reseed. This means that food supply is suddenly greatly reduced. This is a common phenomenon wherever animals graze—if there are too many animals they will strip the land and it will no longer be able to sustain the herd unless there is a rest period of a year or so during which the vegetation is left alone.

Once the crucial point is reached and the land is stripped, the lemmings must look elsewhere for food. In their desperate hungry search, they move in vast numbers across the land. As they move they strip whatever new vegetation they come upon and become more and more desperate. Eventually the survivors reach the sea and, weakened by starvation and perhaps maddened by hunger, some fall in. Although there have been few really careful studies of the phenomenon, it seems very likely that it is the weak and sickly who fall in, not the relatively strong and healthy. Those few lemmings who manage to find food and are still strong do not end up in the ocean unless by chance they are forced in by the rush of the others. In general, those who do survive are the stronger, healthier ones who have found enough food to maintain them, and it is these of course who renew the cycle in the coming years.

A similar phenomenon—a population that increases and then drops sharply—has been observed with other animals in a variety of situations (although without the dramatic jump off the cliff). For example, a herd of sika deer on an isolated island increased rapidly in size and then, instead of stabilizing at some maximum population, decreased precipitously. Forest rangers and game wardens are so familiar with this phenomenon that they watch the size of protected herds very carefully. Instead of allowing the herd to reach its maximum size, they do what is necessary to maintain it at a somewhat lower level. Hunters are allowed to shoot elk and deer in many parts of the United States even though the animals are normally protected by law. The length of the hunting season and the number of permits is adjusted so that enough animals will be killed to stabilize the population. This also occurs in the game preserves in Africa, where wardens are forced to shoot hippopotami and other animals to prevent sharp, destructive fluctuations in their populations.

In unprotected, natural environments, this culling of the weaker members is usually done by predators and disease. When predators are eliminated or climatic and food conditions are overly favorable, this natural selection does not occur and herds can become too large. This can result in an infestation by the animals, who then expand their territory and either destroy the land or drive out less successful animals. When rabbits were introduced into Australia, they found no natural predators and soon multiplied so that they became a threat to man's food supply. If there had been insufficient food for the rabbits, the typical sharp drop in their population would presumably have occurred as soon as the food was exhausted.

In their natural domain most animal populations do not go through these sharp fluctuations. Ordinarily the population is maintained at about the same size by the supply of food and other resources. When it gets a little too large, there is not enough food and some of the animals die or migrate. In unnatural situations such as being isolated on an island or being introduced into a strange environment, the delicate balance is disturbed. Then, the population can rapidly become much too large, thus destroying the food supply and producing the equally sudden decline. The lemmings are in this sense an unusual although probably not unique instance of animals in the regular range who experience these cycles. It does seem clear that the cause of the fluctuation, at least under most circumstances, is the availability of resources, chiefly food. There are years of plenty, during which the population increases, and years of famine, during which it declines. Particularly when the animals have few natural predators, when the food supply and other physical factors such as climate are the main controls on population size, these fluctuations can be very sharp.

Thus, the lemmings do not commit suicide because of overpopulation. They and other animals who experience population cycles of this sort are affected primarily by the supply of resources. Nevertheless, this is not a reason to reject entirely the idea that population density itself can have powerful effects. There are other instances in which dramatic occurrences that coincide with increases in population cannot be explained simply in terms of lack of food. It does seem that under some circumstances the interactions among the individuals or the competition for space have a major impact on the animals. Charles Southwick, John Calhoun, John Christian, and others have studied this phenomenon in the laboratory. With minor variations the procedures for these studies are the same: A number of animals are placed in an enclosed space, given all the food and water they need, and then left alone and observed. A colony might start with four male and six female rats, for whom there is plenty of space. Within this comfortable protected environment the colony thrives. Rats are very good at reproducing, and pretty soon the size of the colony is increasing rapidly. Before too long there are a vast number of animals in the cage. At some point, just as in natural environments, the colony ceases to increase in size and then very suddenly begins to decline. The population drops sharply and there is even some indication that the colony might die out entirely, although none of the experiments have been allowed to continue long enough to see whether this would happen.

This pattern of rapid increase in population followed by a sharp decrease does not occur every time. In a recent study by Kessler a colony of mice increased in size but for some reason the high density did not interfere with the mice's normal behavior. They managed to survive and to reproduce the way they would under less dense circumstances. This variation, although the reason for it is still unclear, does suggest that there may be substantial differences among strains of rodents and therefore among different species. It also indicates that minor variations in the setup of the cage may eliminate the negative effect.

Despite some exceptions, a severe drop in the population of enclosed colonies is the usual pattern, and the question is why this severe drop occurs. It obviously cannot be due to a lack of food or to other aversive natural conditions such as temperature, disease, or predators, as these conditions are all carefully controlled. The decline must be due to the animals themselves. What happens in the cage as the population increases?

When there are relatively few animals in a colony, they live in what might be called their normal style of life. To a rat this means finding one or more mates, building a nest, producing young, and raising them. Each male collects a small harem, designates a section of the cage as his territory, and mates only with the females in his own harem. The males roam fairly freely around the whole cage but do not invade other males' nests, do not mate with other females, do not fight very much among themselves, and generally live a comfortable, productive life. The females concentrate on building an adequate nest, gathering paper, straw, and other soft substances so that the young will have a comfortable bed. The females stay at home more than the males, do not fight, and resist any advances from males of other nests. Once the young are born, the females raise them for some weeks and then are ready to have another litter. Young males roam around the cage interacting with other males, engaging in some minor fighting while they are looking for mates. Once they have found mates, they start a new cycle by building their own nests, collecting their own harem, and so on.

When the population becomes very large, this normal pattern of behavior tends to break down. A few very tough males manage to continue the normal life style. They build nests, collect harems, and manage to protect the nests from other males. These little families manage to produce healthy offspring and thereby add to the population of the colony. But this becomes increasingly difficult and rare as the population increases. Instead, most males are unable to or simply no longer care to establish a nest. Many who do find a home are not strong enough to protect it from other males. The marauding males enter the nests, attack the females, and break up the carefully prepared beds. The females are so harassed by the marauders that they do not prepare adequate nesting for the young, cannot care for the young sufficiently, and cannot protect them when they are vulnerable. The marauders are males who cannot build nests and who instead rush around the cage aggressively attacking other males and females. They engage in promiscuous sexual and homosexual behavior and generally make life difficult for those around them.

Another pattern is for some males to become recluses. They find a small corner of the cage where they are unlikely to be bothered, do not seek mates, and do not engage in any sexual activities. Instead, they sit by themselves, eat and drink enough to sustain them, and manage to stay out of fights. These sleek, well-groomed creatures, whom Calhoun calls "the beautiful ones," manage to survive in the environment but are not active members of the society. They do not produce any young, nor do they interact in the way that rats normally do. Of course, in a way their adaptation is perfect. They may not be behaving normally, but they are surviving and not being hurt. Yet their form of survival is certainly not productive.

On the other hand, they are considerably better off than another group of animals who might be called the apathetic street fighters, or juvenile delinquents. This is the largest group in the colony. It consists of males and some females who gather in large groups without any nests, sometimes milling around on the floor of the cage, sometimes sleeping, and sometimes spontaneously engaging in severe fighting. They do not seek mates, although they do indulge in promiscuous and indiscriminate sexual behavior. These are the weaker creatures who are not strong enough to build their own nests or active enough to become marauders, but are not withdrawn enough to become recluses. They tend to get badly scarred by the endless series of pointless battles. They live out their lives without having a family or even a home.

The immediate cause of the decline in population that is brought about by these conditions is a sharp increase in infant mortality. Even though many of the animals are upset and act peculiarly, and despite the breakdown in normal social and sexual behavior, there are about the usual number of pregnancies. There may be a slight increase in miscarriages and irregular births, but it is not an important factor. On the other hand, there is a catastrophic change in the health of the newborn and young animals. Even under normal conditions many do not reach adulthood. As with any animal that produces large and frequent litters, nature seems to have arranged things so that only the relatively strong survive. But under these crowded circumstances, the mortality rate among the young more than doubles, and despite the rodents' high rate of reproduction, this rate of survival is simply not high enough to maintain a constant population. Too few new, healthy adults are available to mate and produce litters, and accordingly the population drops sharply.

There are large differences in the survival rate of the young among the types of animals used in these experiments. The powerful, dominant males, who build and defend regular nests, produce healthy young who have a more or less normal rate of survival. The other males produce just about as many young, but practically all of them die when they are very young. The reason for this is not complicated or subtle. It is simply that a young rat or mouse needs good care for a while in order to survive. It needs a comfortable, soft nest, a mother that has the time and energy to nurse it, and protection from other animals that might deliberately or inadvertently harm it. Since only the dominant males have such nests, only their offspring have a reasonable chance of growing up to be vigorous, productive members of the rodent society.

It does not appear that the other animals break down entirely. All females who are pregnant attempt to build nests and to nurse and protect their young when they are born. But they are faced with insurmountable difficulties. In the first place, they do not have a good location for a nest. The dominant males have laid claim to the best nesting spots. More important, the males to whom the females would usually look for protection are not strong enough to defend their nests. Neither of these factors would be crucial under less crowded conditions. The females could make do with less than perfect housing if necessary, and nests generally are not invaded very much by strangers anyway. Unfortunately, the huge number of animals in the small space makes life much more difficult. Even if they were not trying to invade and upset nests, the other animals would tend to wander into them simply by chance. There is very little space, so when a rat wants to take a walk or even just turn around, he can hardly avoid encroaching on some other rat's private territory. Whether or not any of this is done deliberately, it does seem to be an inevitable result of the lack of space. Except for those animals that have built and can defend an adequate nest and those who are recluses, all of the rats mill around in the remaining space and must interfere with each other. The most crucial aspect of that interference is trampling on nests and harming the young. There is some cannibalism, but very little—the marauders and strollers do not seem to be deliberately attacking the young. Rather, they interfere with their normal upbringing almost by chance simply because there is too little space.

Thus, the nests are inadequate to begin with because there is too little space to build them; the weaker males are not strong enough to protect them from the unusually high rate of incursions; the females are upset by all of this and do a less good job of caring for their young; and the marauders trample the nest and harm the young in the process. All of this adds up to a very bad home life, and most of the animals do not survive.

In addition to the breakdown in normal nesting behavior and the resulting increase in infant mortality, high density appears to produce increased aggressiveness, sexual promiscuity, cannibalism, and for some individuals withdrawal from life. The juvenile delinquents who engage in senseless fighting are not vying for mates or nesting space, but attacking each other for no apparent reason. Although under low density conditions rats will always fight strangers and will sometimes even fight familiar rats, the levels are considerably lower than under high density. Careful observations and control groups are lacking, but it also appears that there is a higher level of homosexuality and indiscriminate mating under high density. Anecdotal reports describe the males as more sexually aggressive than usual, forcing themselves on uninterested females. Cannibalism is rare even under high density, but, at least according to Calhoun, it is higher than usual. And the phenomenon of some animals withdrawing from social interaction has been reported only under high density, although again this is highly anecdotal, with no good comparison groups. Despite the absence of controls in some of this research, the evidence is quite convincing that high density produces an overall breakdown in normal social behavior.

Research also indicates that living under conditions of high density with a large number of other animals has some specific physiological effects, particularly on adrenal activity. Since the adrenal gland grows larger as it becomes more active, its size is an excellent measure of adrenal activity. Deer who were stranded on an island under conditions of high density were found to have abnormally large adrenal glands. Similar findings have been reported for other animals under naturally occurring high density circumstances.

Controlled laboratory research has produced similar findings. Rats were put in cages containing one, two, four, ten, or twenty animals, and their adrenal glands were measured at the end of a week. It was found that animals in cages containing ten or twenty other rats had larger adrenals than those who had been in cages with fewer animals or by themselves. This has been confirmed in a number of careful studies using various animals and cage sizes.

Similar research has been conducted on the sexual organs of male rats, but the evidence here is less consistent. An occasional study found a decrease in the size of testes corresponding to the number of rats in the cage, one found a decrease in the size of the seminal vesicles, and one reported a decrease in the number of spermatozoa in rats who were in cages with larger groups, but there are a number of reports of no differences in any of these measures.

The fascinating and important aspect of this laboratory work is that the amount of space available to the rats seems to be almost irrelevant. When ten rats are put in a cage three feet by three feet, their adrenal glands are larger than those of a rat who is by himself in a cage one foot by one foot, even though the rats in the two cages have about the same amount of space (one square foot per rat). When the size of the cage containing the ten rats is increased to five feet by five feet, allowing each rat two and one-half square feet, the adrenal glands increase even though the rats now have more space than the rat in the individual cage. In fact, it has even been shown that making the cage thirty-two times as large does not change the results—ten rats in that huge cage still have larger adrenal glands than one rat in a very small cage. In other words, it does not appear to be the amount of space that is crucial but rather the number of animals in the cage.

This seems to imply that it is not crowding that produces the increased adrenal activity; it is having to interact with all those other animals. This makes perfectly good sense. A rat alone in a small cage is exposed to very little stimulation, very little stress, very little excitement. If he were alone in a larger cage, very much the same would be true. In contrast, a rat who has to deal with nine other rats in the same cage is constantly interacting with them, competing with them for food (or perhaps to get first nibble even if there is plenty of food to go around), bumping into them, gossiping, making friends, and so on. There is lots of activity, lots of action, lots of interaction. This is true whether the cage is small or large. As long as the cage is small enough so that all the animals tend to interact, the size should not make much difference. This has been succinctly summarized by D. A. Rodgers and D. D. Thiessen: "The effects on the adrenal gland appear to be independent of the amount of space available per animal."

Studies on the effects of group rearing on susceptibility to disease, although not directly related to this issue, offer an interesting comparison. Once again the cages contain from one to twenty rats. At some point in their lives all of the animals are injected with a virus or with disease-causing bacteria. The primary measure of susceptibility is how soon the animals die or how many die by a certain time. Unfortunately there is not enough research to provide definitive answers, but it seems quite clear that there are no consistent effects of group rearing on susceptibility to disease. With some diseases, the group-reared animals are more susceptible—that is, more of them catch the disease and die more quickly than do animals in cages containing fewer animals or single animals. With some diseases, exactly the reverse is true—animals who are in large groups are less susceptible to disease, live longer, and die less quickly. There is some evidence that the effects are very complicated and depend to some extent on the exact dosage of the bacteria or virus, the particular disease, and even the strain of rat used. In other words being in a large group does not make the rat either more or less immune to disease. This is also true of rats who were exposed to conditions likely to produce ulcers. Group-reared rats were, if anything, less likely to develop ulcers than were rats in cages containing fewer animals or those alone in a cage.

Finally, there is evidence on the effects of density on emotionality of animals. Typical signs of emotionality in a rat are responding to stimulation by freezing, defecating, urinating, or running erratically. A rat who is moving quietly about the cage, sniffing in the corners, occasionally grooming himself, licking his paws, nuzzling up to another rat, pawing at the bars, and nibbling food would be considered fairly calm. In contrast, a rat who crouches unmoving for a long time (assuming he wasn't sleeping), throws himself against the bars, defecates a great deal, or runs quickly to and fro would be considered emotional. There are fairly standard, reliable tests of emotionality in rats that involve observations as well as objective measures.

The research on emotionality has followed the same pattern as the work on adrenal and gonadal activity. The majority of the studies have found that group-reared animals are less emotional, but some have found that they are more emotional. Although it is somewhat misleading merely to count the number of studies on each side, at the moment it seems safe to say that being raised in a group does not in general make animals more emotional. It may have this effect under certain, as yet unspecified conditions, but by and large group-reared animals appear to be less (not more) emotional than animals who have been raised alone.

In a way, this makes good sense. Animals who have been raised with other animals have been exposed to a great deal of stimulation and presumably have to some extent adapted to it. The animal who is raised alone is exposed to almost no stimulation and does not know how to cope with it when it comes along. Thus, the group-reared animal, who lives in a situation of greater excitement and apparently has a more active adrenal gland, is actually less emotional than the animal raised individually.

To summarize the results of crowding on animals:

1. At a certain point the population declines sharply.

2. There is greatly increased infant mortality caused primarily by inadequate nest building and care of the young by the females.

3. There is increased aggressiveness and a breakdown in normal social behavior.

4. Some animals become recluses and no longer engage in any social behavior.

5. The strongest animals survive and are able to breed, raise young, and in general live a normal life.

6. Adrenal activity is increased and male gonadal activity somewhat decreased by exposure to larger numbers of other animals, but density is relatively unimportant.

7. Emotionality and susceptibility to disease are not generally negatively affected.

ANIMAL THEORIES

Various attempts have been made to explain the effects of crowding on animals. One explanation, which has achieved considerable popularity in the works of Robert Ardrey and Konrad Lorenz, is that animals want and need a certain amount of space around them. They regard this space as their own and have proprietary and protective attitudes toward it. These attitudes and the reactions they engender have been termed *territoriality*. When their territory is encroached upon, the animals feel threatened and have an instinctive tendency to attack the trespasser. When there is adequate space, the individual's territory will not be encroached upon and the animals can live together peacefully. As the space gets smaller, feelings of territoriality are aroused and aggression automatically occurs. This increased aggression causes fighting, which harms the animals, results in shorter life spans, interferes with child rearing, and produces increased infant mortality. In other words, this theory proposes a direct link between reduced space and aggressiveness, with the aggressiveness in turn producing all the other effects noted.

There is considerable anecdotal evidence that, under appropriate circumstances, something resembling territoriality does occur. Most of the stories involve situations in which an animal's nest or home territory has been encroached upon by strangers. For example, Konrad Lorenz provides a beautiful description of a tropical fish, a Beau Gregory, attacking members of his own species who invade his hunting ground, searching for food. The first Beau "sees the intruder later than I do from my lookout post, and he only notices him when he is within about four yards. Then he shoots toward him furiously, whereupon the stranger, although he is a little bigger than his adversary, switches around and flees with vigorous strokes in wild zigzags, trying to avoid the ramming movements of his pursuer. . . . As soon as the stranger has disappeared into the dusky blue-green distance, the victor returns to his hollow, treading his way calmly through a dense shoal of young grunts who are in search of food in front of the entrance." This fish attacked a member of his own species, but not any other fish.

The same phenomenon occurs with many other animals. The original owner of a hunting area will attack a newcomer and drive it off. A pride of lions has a very large hunting ground but will do whatever it can to drive off other hunting lions from the area. As soon as a strange lion approaches, the largest males in the pride will rush over, their fur bristling, emitting furious roars, and obviously threatening to attack. According to most ethologists, these encounters rarely end in an actual battle. The roaring and strutting about of the homeowner is done mainly as a threat rather than a call to a fight. The interloper usually retreats and no fighting occurs. But if for some reason there were no other place to go (in an experiment or where there is severe competition for hunting areas), presumably some sort of fight would occur, with the loser abandoning the territory.

This phenomenon can also be observed in dogs. A dog walking along the street stops to play when he meets another dog. There is almost always mutual nuzzling and fairly friendly interaction. Occasionally dogs will fight on the street but that is the exception. In contrast, a dog in his own backyard tends to be extremely protective. A strange dog passing by will not be greeted with friendship but rather will be warned off by fierce growlings and baring of the teeth. And any dog intrepid enough to enter a strange backyard is likely to be attacked, even if the dog owning the yard is much smaller. Dogs that are already friends are welcomed, but strangers are immediately made aware that this is home territory and not to be encroached upon. It is also true that a dog being attacked by other dogs may run from them, but as soon as he reaches home he will turn around and fight. At that point he is protecting his own territory and seems, all of a sudden, to have an enormous advantage; not only is he made fierce and brave by being at home, but the other dogs tend to be cowed by being in the other's territory. Each dog defends his own territory and the others tend to respect it. This is all anecdotal, of course, but virtually any dog lover can provide similar stories.

In *Never Cry Wolf*, Farley Mowat, who lived for several months among the giant timberwolves in Canada, describes the ritual with which wolves map out their own hunting territory. A male wolf makes the rounds of his territory urinating at various points along the border, just as men might erect flags. Mowat eventually went around leaving similar marks to insure a certain amount of territory for himself. Although this method of marking boundaries has the slight disadvantage of needing to be renewed every once in a while, it is certainly very simple compared to the elaborate machinery humans usually use, and at least among the wolves, as long as there is enough hunting space these boundaries appear to be respected by other members of the species.

Almost all animals seem to display territorial behavior under some circumstances. They will protect a certain amount of territory and act aggressively toward any member of the same species attempting to intrude on it. There is no arguing about this, but the important question is whether this behavior is due to instinctive need for territory. It is known that animals sometimes react aggressively when they are crowded, and a territorial instinct would account for this behavior. Otherwise, the idea of territoriality is not an explanation but simply a description of how they behave. It is therefore necessary to look for evidence as to whether or not territoriality is instinctive.

One characteristic of instinctive behavior is that it is not likely to be affected by variations in the situation. If animals behaved aggressively whenever they have little space, regardless of any other factor, their behavior would be evidence that territoriality is instinctive; aggression that occurs only when certain other factors are also present would be evidence against instinct.

As Konrad Lorenz and others have pointed out, staking out a territory and then protecting it from intrusion by others of the same species is very sensible behavior, as there is only a certain amount of food available in any given area. If too many wolves or lions or tropical fish of the same species tried to find food in the same corner of the forest or the ocean, there would not be enough for them to live on. Although the wolves in Canada eat an occasional caribou or elk, they live mostly on small rodents such as rats and mice. Obviously, the number of wolves that can find food in any one area is limited by the number of rodents in that area. Presumably, the hunting area that each family of wolves marks out is approximately large enough to sustain the family. If the area is shared with another family of wolves, hunting will become difficult and eventually some or all the wolves will starve. Therefore, driving away other wolves is adaptive behavior which serves to enable the wolves to survive.

Clearly, this kind of behavior will have survival value only when food is limited. The more food there is in a given area, the more animals it can support and, accordingly, the less necessary it is for the wolves to drive off other wolves. In the very cold areas of northern Canada and Alaska, there are relatively few rodents and virtually no caribou, and therefore a given area may be able to support only ten wolves. Farther south, where there are more rodents and large game, the same amount of land may support two or three times as many wolves. In an extreme case, where there is unlimited food (such as in a zoo or in a controlled experiment), there is no reason in terms of food supply to limit the number of animals in a given area.

If territoriality is instinctive, it should not disappear even when food supply is unlimited. If it is an instinctive, innate reaction of the organism, if animals "need" a certain amount of space and will defend it from others, this should occur whether or not food is available. True, it will have greater adaptive and survival value when food is limited, but it should occur under all circumstances. Although there is very little direct evidence bearing on this question, it seems quite clear that the presence of ample amounts of food and water greatly reduces and perhaps eliminates entirely any territorial response.

Under circumstances in which a limited amount of food is available, many animals do exhibit the kind of behavior that has been called territoriality. The animals map out an area for themselves and will do what they can to drive off other animals of the same species who attempt to invade it. But this does not seem to occur when food is readily available, does not occur by any means with all animals, and almost certainly is not directly related to the amount of space available but rather to other factors.

Anyone who has ever seen a cage full of rats should be immediately aware that rats do not dislike physical contact. When they sleep, which is often, they will almost inevitably curl up all together in one corner of the cage. This cuddling is not necessarily a sexual thing. In cages of all males and all females the rats will cuddle together in much the same way. A walk through a zoo will supply evidence of this obvious preference for physical contact among most species. Even in huge cages, the bears will be lying all over each other, the lions will be curled up together in a corner, the monkeys, the wolves, the muskrats, the raccoons and just about every other animal, regardless of the number in the cage, will huddle together rather than avoid physical contact. Admittedly, these cages are not terribly cramped and presumably the animals have had a chance to get to know one another, but obviously they have much less space here than they do in the wilds and at least to begin with most of the animals were strangers.

A friend of mine told me of a study he had done in which two rats were raised together almost from birth and then a new rat was put in the cage. The two friendly rats fought constantly with the interloper; it was their cage and apparently they resented his joining them. But this hardly seems to be a case of territoriality, since the three slept huddled together at night even though they were fighting during the day. It seems that one can dislike a newcomer for a variety of reasons, quite independent of his invasion of your territory. Far from needing a certain amount of space around them which they do not want other animals to invade, rats will huddle together even with an enemy. This may be an extreme example, but anyone who works with animals must know that in virtually all situations they seek out rather than avoid physical contact with other members of their species.

This is not to say that one group of animals, for example a pack of baboons, will take kindly to another pack of baboons coming too close to them. Separate packs of animals often do try to preserve a certain amount of space for themselves. But this seems to be more a case of rivalry or perhaps protecting their children and home or hunting ground rather than an instinctive need to preserve a certain amount of territory or an aggressive response triggered by another animal getting too close.

Once again, the crucial question is whether the aggressiveness sometimes shown toward other members of the species is dependent on the amount of space available. If it is directly dependent on the amount of space, then it would seem to be a clear instance of territoriality: the animal attacks when the space he is protecting is trespassed upon. If the amount of space is largely irrelevant, a much simpler explanation would be that the animal is quite sensibly protecting his young, his mate, his supply of food, or whatever else he considers necessary for survival. As long as these are protected, he will not attack. If this is the case, he is not responding to invasions of territory but rather to actual threats, and that is quite a different story.

For some reason there has been extremely little research specifically directed to the question of how the amount of space available affects animal behavior. As already mentioned, studies have shown that when a colony of rats and mice is allowed to increase in size within a given area, there is a marked increase in aggressiveness, and in a sense, social breakdown eventually does occur. But since the amount of space did not vary separately from the number of animals, it might be argued that the same kind of effects might have occurred even if there were considerably more space available. In other words, effects may be due to the huge number of animals rather than a decrease in the amount of space available per animal. In a study (Myers *et al.*) of rabbits that did vary both number and density, the result was that both factors increased aggressiveness. This suggests that at least under some conditions for some animals the amount of space is the crucial factor producing the negative effects, but thus far this has been shown by only one experiment.

In experiments in which animals are confined for relatively short periods of time and their behavior and physiological responses observed, the findings seem to be inconsistent with an instinctive notion of territoriality. The most important result is that being in a cage with other animals produces effects regardless of the size of the cage. Animals in groups have larger adrenal glands, are generally more active, and are less emotional than those that are alone. But all of this is independent of the amount of space available. Five rats in a small cage do not differ from five rats in a much larger cage. If a territorial instinct were operating, the amount of space would be crucial, and it is not.

Furthermore, it is far from clear that the effects of being in a group, even when crowded, are negative. On the contrary, being in a group with very little space makes the animals less emotional than individual animals who have lots of space and has no adverse effects on their health. Adrenal glands are larger in groups, but it may be that isolated rats have abnormally small adrenals rather than that grouped animals have overly large ones. In general, this research strongly suggests that space is a less critical variable than whether or not the animal is in a group and the size of the group. If there were an instinctive need for space, reducing the area would have clearly negative effects, and it does not.

To be fair, it does seem as if the effects of crowding depend to some extent on the species or even on the particular variety of that species. Perhaps some creatures do have strong territorial instincts that operate regardless of other factors in the situation while others do not. There is ample evidence that most species can compress the amount of territory they normally occupy without suffering ill effects, but some are probably more sensitive than others. In controlled experiments, rabbits seem to respond especially badly to lack of space, while rats and mice are less negatively affected. In their natural habitat, some animals appear to be more aware of space and territory than others. Within the same species they are sometimes "territorial" and sometimes not. For example, the brown bear has been observed to defend territory under some conditions and not under others; elk have group territories in one area and are indifferent to territory in another.

The reasons for believing that most animals do not have a territorial instinct are: First, animals seem to like physical contact. This is anecdotal evidence, but it suggests that there is no instinctive need for the individual animals to have a certain amount of space around them. It leaves open the possibility that a group or family needs a minimum amount of space or that under some circumstances the individual will also react to a lack of space.

Second, controlled studies on reactions to lack of space have produced mixed results. Reducing space while holding number constant sometimes increased aggressiveness, sometimes not. If there is an instinct, the results should be consistent, as an instinct is always in operation and does not vary from situation to situation. These results suggest, therefore, either that no instinct exists or that it is found only in certain species. They also indicate that other factors in the situation are much more important in determining behavior than is a need for territory.

Finally, the experiments on relatively short-term confinement demonstrate that the amount of space has little or no effect, while the number of other animals present does. Once again, if there were an instinctive territorial reaction, animals in smaller areas should show more negative responses. That they do not argues strongly against the instinctive notion.

Therefore, it seems unlikely that animals have built-in instinctive territorial instincts in the sense that Ardrey and others mean it. Some animals may have such an instinct, and many animals probably have it under conditions involving limited food supply or protection of the nest or family. But the evidence seems clear that territorial behavior depends on these other factors and is not absolute. Lack of space by itself does not trigger an aggressive or defensive response, nor does it have other negative effects.

A different explanation of crowding effects has been offered, with some important variations, by J. J. Christian, V. C. Wynne-Edwards, and others. The basic idea of this explanation, known as homeostatic theory, is that animals respond to population density so as to maintain their population at a certain level, or perhaps at a certain level relative to the available resources. Rather than allowing population to increase so much that members of the species will eventually starve to death, various mechanisms operate to keep control of the size of the population. Wynne-Edwards argues that virtually all social institutions and behavior exist in order to control population density. This is such a general notion that it is not particularly helpful to the problem under discussion. Even if some social behavior does have this function, there remains the original job of specifying the mechanisms.

Christian's version of this approach is a sophisticated explanation in physiological terms. He suggests that high density is stressful, that it produces an increase in adrenal activity, and that together these account for all of the effects. This is an ingenious and useful idea, because it attempts to explain the known effects in terms of basic physiological and endocrinal processes. Rather than merely asserting the existence of an instinct, it involves a deeper level of analysis, providing some description of how the effects are produced within the animal. Although it does not seem to account for all of the facts, it does explain some of them very neatly.

To begin with, there is little doubt that, under some circumstances, being with many other animals in a small space is stressful. This is clearly true when there is a shortage of some resource, such as food, water, mates, or nesting space. Even when stress is not produced, being with other animals does increase the individual's activity level. Either stress or activity would be reflected in increased adrenal activity. As already pointed out, there is substantial and consistent evidence that in both natural and experimental situations animals under crowded conditions have larger, more active adrenal glands.

This increased adrenal activity causes, or at least goes along with, a general stepping up of the animal's internal activity. The heart beats faster, metabolism increases, and so on. If extreme enough, it is as if the animal were always "hopped up," always excited and tense. Obviously, in the long run this is not good for health. It may produce heart disease, ulcers, or a number of other physical malfunctions and eventually will probably shorten the animal's life span indirectly or even cause death directly by way of a heart attack or serious ulcer. The first effect of great tension on animals, then, is that they are less healthy and will probably live less long.

The second effect is that animals with high adrenal activity are more excitable and respond less calmly to stimulation. When approached by a rat who is trying to be friendly, an overactive rat might be too jumpy or nervous to accept the friendly overtures and might, instead, respond aggressively. Any additional stress in the situation, such as lack of food or even having to wait on line to get to the food hopper, might trigger an aggressive reaction which would otherwise not occur. This increased aggressiveness would lead to much more fighting. Some animals would get wounded or even killed, and in the long run this would again reduce the life span.

Finally, and most ingeniously, the increased adrenal activity can lead to a decrease in gonadal activity. Overactive adrenal glands tend to be associated with underactive sex glands. Hypertense rats are undersexed rats. This is partly due to a decrease in the production of testosterone (the effects of crowding occur mostly in males) so that the animals have less sex urge. There is also some evidence that there is a decrease in the amount of sperm produced, so that even if they have the sex urge they will be less likely to produce young. Finally, overactive fighting animals are probably less likely to become engaged in love affairs or, at any rate, in successful matings, and accordingly are less likely to become fathers. All of this means that the increased adrenal activity should lead to a decrease in reproductive activity.

Taken together these effects can explain many of the results of overcrowding. The increased aggressiveness observed by Calhoun and others is due to overexcitement and nervousness. The poor nest building could probably be attributed to the same cause. And the decline in population might be due to decrease in sexual activity, infertility, and general unhealthiness. The theory thus accounts for most of the effects and provides a concrete mechanism by which they are produced. In addition, it provides an elegant explanation of how animal populations remain stable. When the population gets too large, overcrowding occurs and produces increased adrenal activity, which in turn causes decreased gonadal activity, which results in a decrease in the population until it is back to the right level.

Unfortunately, although the theory does make a substantial contribution to an understanding of these complex effects, it is not consistent with all the facts and thus is not a full account of the phenomena. As mentioned earlier, the adrenal gland does enlarge under crowded conditions, but the amount of space per animal seems much less important than the number of animals. A large cage with ten animals will produce larger adrenals than a tiny cage with a few animals, even though the smaller cage is much more crowded. This finding does not contradict the idea that adrenal activity is important, but it does argue strongly against the notion that it responds to density.

The homeostatic theory does not fit well with the work on emotionality in rats. As described earlier, rats in large groups are, if anything, less emotional than those raised in isolation or in smaller groups. If crowding caused increased adrenal activity which in turn produced nervousness, the results should be the opposite.

The evidence on susceptibility to disease does not contradict the theory, but it certainly does not support it. Being in a group sometimes increases and sometimes decreases resistance to disease. This depends on many factors, including the type of disease, dosage, and even the strain of animal. Thus, it would be difficult to argue that the susceptibility to disease was a consistent factor producing the decline in population in crowded communities.

Finally, there is no evidence that the crowded animals are any less active sexually. Their style and tastes may be unusual—there is more homosexuality and indiscriminate mating—but there are the normal number of pregnancies and live births. If crowding does produce any decrease in gonadal activity or fertility among some animals, the others apparently make up for it.

In summary, this theory accounts for some but not all of the findings. It provides a beginning point for understanding the physiological mechanism underlying some of the effects, and this is a major contribution. However, it cannot explain all of the consequences of crowding and is inconsistent with some of them. Although the approach is valuable, it is not an adequate theory by itself.

Although each of the explanations discussed previously has something to offer, it does not seem that either of them is totally adequate. Even taken together they cannot account for all of the facts. Something more is needed. I would propose that the effects are due at least in part to problems involved in the social interaction among the animals. Much of the evidence indicates that the number of animals may be more crucial than the amount of space per animal. When there is another animal in the cage or the backyard or the prairie, he must be dealt with. When there are ten others, they must be dealt with. The more there are, the more frequent and intense the social interactions. This increase in interaction level can explain many or all of the effects that have been reported.

The simplest situation is that of the lemmings marching to the sea. Here the presence of the other lemmings presents a serious, straightforward problem—there is simply not enough food to feed all of the animals. The lemmings fight for the food, continually search for new food and eventually cease reproducing, become very aggressive in fighting for the resources, and suffer various kinds of breakdowns due to the lack of food and probably to the strain of the competition; eventually the colony declines sharply in size because the animals starve, no longer reproduce, and fall into the sea. There is nothing subtle in this situation; it is a case of too many animals and not enough food. It does not seem that an endocrine explanation is necessary to account for the effect. When there is not enough food, animals will fight for what is left and many of them will starve. Enough of them survive to start the cycle over again, and next time also the colony will grow too large for the land to sustain and starvation will occur again.

When there are ten animals in a cage rather than one, the most reliable finding is that there is increased adrenal activity, as shown by an increase in the size of the adrenal gland. This increase in adrenal activity can be accounted for by the increase in social interaction, because there is more stimulation when ten animals are present than when there is only one. The animals interact constantly—they play with each other, they bump into each other, they occasionally fight, they make sexual advances to each other, and so on. All of this interaction is stimulating. The animals are more active, more excited, in a sense more alive, and this increase in excitement and activity level will be reflected in increased adrenal activity.

This is quite different from saying that the adrenal increase is due to increased tension or nervousness. As already noted, the evidence shows that animals raised in groups are less emotional and nervous than those raised alone. This finding is consistent with the social-interaction theory. The presence of other animals is stimulating but, except under circumstances where they constitute a threat, not tension-producing. The increase in adrenal activity is therefore not an indication of an increase in emotionality.

The evidence on susceptibility to disease is also consistent with the social-interaction theory. If the presence of other animals produced tension, animals in groups would be more susceptible to disease, would get ulcers more easily, and would have shorter life spans. If, however, the presence of other animals is stimulating without being tension-producing, there is no reason to expect any consistent effects on susceptibility to disease—and no such consistent effects have been found.

Finally, consider the effects that occur when a colony of animals in a laboratory is allowed to increase greatly in size. When the cage contained twenty, thirty, forty, or even one hundred animals, they all seemed lively, healthy, and normal. They built nests, raised their young, and acted the way rats or mice are expected to act. But when the population of the cage became much greater—hundreds of animals in the enclosed area—there was an increase in aggressiveness, a decrease in nest building, and a general social breakdown. At that point the population stopped increasing and dropped sharply, primarily due to extremely high infant mortality because of inadequate nest building and care of the young.

This phenomenon also appears to be caused primarily by the intensified social interaction and in particular by the competition for a scarce resource. What is that scarce resource? Obviously space. Although those who have done this work describe the cage as being large enough to hold and sustain more animals than it actually contains even at the highest point of population, this is somewhat misleading. True, there is enough space in the cage for hundreds of animals to be able to have four feet on the floor—but animals need more space than that to build a nest. In addition, they much prefer an area that is in a corner or that is at least against a wall. Thus, a cage offers a limited number of good locations for a nest. Even if the rats were willing to build nests in the middle of the floor, they would need some means to keep pedestrian traffic away from their nests, and rats have not generally learned to build this kind of nest.

Now, if colonies are examined from this point of view,

it becomes clear that the inability either to find a place to build a nest or to build one is the most important single cause of the social breakdown. The few particularly strong males who do find the best spots and do build nests lead more or less normal lives. These males are lucky enough and strong enough to get a corner or some other ideal nesting location. They build nests, mate with some females, raise young, and generally lead normal, healthy, productive lives. In each of the colonies some males manage to do this regardless of the number of animals in the cage, but as the population increases, it becomes more and more difficult for any male to find and protect an adequate nest. This need not be because the animals are instinctively or naturally terribly aggressive or because they have suffered a social breakdown. Rather, it is that there are very few good spots for nests and a great deal of competition for them. Presumably, only the strongest males will be able to find good locations. In addition, as the population grows, the number of good locations actually decreases. When there are very few animals in the cage, even a fairly unsheltered nest might be adequate. When there are a great many animals in the cage, a nest needs to be sheltered so that it will not be overrun by animals passing to and fro or simply walking around sightseeing.

Animals who cannot build adequate nests simply cannot lead normal lives. A rat is a fairly simple creature. In a colony of rats there is one fairly straightforward, structured way of living. Each male finds a place to build a nest, attracts a number of females, mates with them, and then defends the nest while the young are born. If a rat cannot lead his life this way, he has few alternatives in his behavioral repertoire. He is, in a sense, cut out to be a father and nest builder; the females are cut out to be part of a harem, to bear young, and to take care of them. Other than foraging for food, exploring a little, and occasionally playing with other animals of the species, that is the rat's destiny.

If this way of living is interfered with—that is, if a rat is deprived of a home—it is not surprising that he becomes disoriented and disturbed. There is not much left for him to do. That is why the animals who are unable to build nests simply mill around in a disoriented, confused manner. As the number of the dispossessed, disoriented animals increases, there is more and more confusion in the colony, causing even more rats to become disoriented, and so on.

When a large number of humans is suddenly dispossessed because of war or some natural disaster, they too have difficulty adjusting. In a refugee camp, every family tries to establish a tiny home, sometimes by hanging a blanket between itself and the next family or even by putting a string around an area to claim it as theirs. When there are individuals who are not members of families, there is a great deal of disorientation and disturbance because they do not have a place of their own to sleep and to establish themselves. Fortunately for humans, they have available to them a vast repertoire of behavior, are very adaptable, and are able to cope with situations in a flexible way, besides which they can cooperate among themselves (when they want to) and try to bring order out of what would otherwise be chaos. The purpose of the comparison is not to generalize about humans on the basis of experiments on rats, but to show that even for humans such a situation would be difficult, and thus to emphasize how difficult it must be for the rats.

The effects found in the crowded-colony experiments may be due to competition for the limited resource of space and, more particularly, competition for room to build a nest. The animals do not need a certain amount of space around them, they do not instinctively become aggressive when there is very little space, they do not suffer social breakdowns simply because the nest is crowded; it is when they are unable to build a nest and live a normal life that they suffer disorientation and eventually a complete social breakdown. It is not anything mysterious, not an instinctive need for territory, not simply a dramatic increase in adrenal activity, but rather a perfectly natural reaction to the inability to lead normal lives. If the cage were arranged so that each animal could build an adequate nest and the nests were easily protected from other animals, these dramatic effects might not occur and the colonies would continue to grow in size until there was no longer space for adequate nest building.

To repeat the social-interaction explanation of the effects of crowding on animals other than humans: Crowding, or simply the presence of a large number of other animals, acts primarily as an intensifier of the social interaction. When there are sufficient resources, this results in increased stimulation, excitement, and general activity level. It will accordingly produce an increase in adrenal activity but will not produce an increase in emotionality or a decrease in health. However, the presence of a large number of other animals will intensify the competition for any scarce resource, whether it be food, space, or anything else.

In summary, the effects of high density and large populations on animals are probably due to a variety of factors. Some animals may have territorial instincts, and others may respond with territorial behavior under certain limited circumstances. But there is little evidence for a universal or automatic territorial response, and it is not an adequate explanation of the density effects. Some of the effects are probably due directly to the increase in adrenal activity. When high density occurs in the absence of sufficient resources, dealing with the other animals is difficult and stressful. This produces tension, possibly increased aggressiveness, and conceivably decreased sexual activity, although there is little evidence for the last. Finally, the presence of other animals and an increase in density intensifies social interactions. Ordinarily this is stimulating without being stressful, but when resources are scarce the competition is also intensified, and this produces negative effects.

FROM MICE TO MEN?

It is both difficult and risky to generalize directly from the behavior of one animal to that of another. It would be a mistake to conclude that dogs act a particular way just because cats do or that monkeys act the same way as lions, and it is of course much more difficult to conclude anything about humans from other animals. Humans are more intelligent, have language, and have an extremely complex social structure, are much more flexible and innovative than other animals, have a history which they can remember, and so on. This is not to say that there is a discontinuity between humans and other animals—humans are animals and have much in common with the others—but there is enough difference between humans and the rest of the animal world to make it difficult to conclude anything about humans from what other animals do. Even if every other animal behaved in a particular way, this would not justify drawing the firm conclusion that humans behave the same way.

Nevertheless, work on animals is not only extremely interesting but can also be a source of ideas and suggestions about how humans behave. Everything that can be learned about the rest of the animal world is useful in understanding humans. First, it puts human behavior in perspective, showing how humans are different and how they are the same. It makes it possible to begin to see the place of humans in the world relative to other animals, to begin to understand how humans' greater intelligence and other attributes make human behavior different from—or in some cases the same as—that of other animals. This shows not only man's uniqueness (when he is different) but also his position in the animal hierarchy (when he acts like other animals). Secondly, knowing how other animals behave provides hints as to how humans may behave. Students of human behavior need hunches, guesses, something on which to base observations and theories. Of course, once human beings have been thoroughly studied, conclusions can be based on the results of observation. But until that study is complete (which presumably is a long way off), knowledge of other animals can provide a basis for some hypotheses. For most purposes, it is easier, quicker, and more efficient to study other animals than to study humans. Because rats reproduce very rapidly, it is possible to study a series of generations of rats and a colony that grows enormously in size over a few years. Obviously, the same experiment with humans (even if it were morally, ethically, and legally possible) would take hundreds of years. This is only one example of how the work of ethologists, biologists, and psychologists on nonhumans is extremely helpful in the study of humans.

Unfortunately, there has been a tendency in recent years to draw conclusions about human behavior directly from the behavior of other animals. This is a grave mistake. It is always misleading, often foolish. Even Konrad Lorenz, the Nobel Prize-winning ethologist, has had a tendency in recent years to make broad statements about human behavior based on his studies of tropical fish. And when men such as Desmond Morris, Lionel Tiger, and Robert Ardrey write whole books in which they make profound statements about humans based on other animals, it is truly disheartening. Sadly, the American public devours books of this kind in great numbers and, presumably, swallows whole many of the conclusions.

One of the assumptions that many ethologists start from is that any characteristic of an animal must be there for a good reason. They base this belief on a misinterpretation of the Darwinian notion of selection, which is that characteristics with high survival value will be retained because those members of the species having them will tend to survive. Over many generations a new characteristic with high survival value that appears in a few members of the species will tend to become common to all members of the species. This explanation of why some new attributes remain and others vanish is extremely powerful and useful but Darwinian theory does not require that every characteristic that exists have high survival value. All it says is that characteristics with very high survival value will tend to be retained and those with very low survival value will tend to disappear. It leaves open the possibility that many characteristics that are relatively unimportant in terms of survival may or may not be retained, partly on the basis of chance and partly because of mechanisms that are not yet understood.

It seems foolish to argue that every single characteristic of the species must be there for a good reason or that every aspect of an animal must have high survival value. It is particularly foolish to argue that the exact combination of characteristics appearing in a particular species is *the* best combination that could possibly have occurred. Almost all adolescent human males have a tendency to develop acne but I don't think anyone would suggest that this characteristic is there because it has high survival value. There are physiological reasons why most humans are right-handed, but surely it would be better in terms of survival for humans to be totally ambidextrous. Virtually all humans have exactly five toes on each foot and four fingers and a thumb on each hand. We are quite used to this and we are able to walk well on our five toes and manipulate tools well with our hands. But it would be difficult to argue that this is the best possible arrangement of toes and fingers. Perhaps an extra few toes would lead to greater stability; an opposing thumb on the foot (as some of the primates have) would allow us to do tasks with our feet that we can now only do with our hands; two opposing thumbs on each hand would make our grips stronger and surer; and so on. It is not that we need additional fingers or toes or thumbs, but they probably would come in handy.

And imagine having a prehensile tail! Just think of all the tasks that could be performed by a long, thin tail which was highly maneuverable and manipulable. Although generally there is no reason for us to swing through trees or hang upside down from a branch, it might be nice to be able to do so. Think of those times when it would be nice to have a third hand to carry an extra package or to defend oneself in a fight. A long tail could serve this purpose and at the same time add stability and serve as an additional source of protection from the rear. It might also be the basis of a whole new industry providing decorations for the tail, special bows, clothing, and so on. It is hard to argue that man is better off because he doesn't have a tail. True the lack of a tail may have forced him into certain roles which have led to his eventual development—but it would be even better if he were as developed as he is and had a tail to boot.

It is a grave mistake to conclude that simply because an animal has survived up to this point, he is as well suited as he could possibly be or that every characteristic of the animal is to the good. Some characteristics have survival value, some do not, and some interfere with the animal's functioning. The search for the reasons for the existence of every single characteristic is thus often fruitless. It sometimes leads otherwise good scientists to stretch the facts and logic in order to justify a trait that does not have a justification in terms of survival.

It is a general weakness of the ethological approach to the study of man that too much emphasis is placed on explaining why a particular trait exists rather than on exact descriptions of how man functions or malfunctions. There is a tendency to accept *Homo sapiens* as a perfectly functioning entity, with every characteristic fulfilling some purpose for the ultimate good of the species. It has led, in part, to the idea that human birthrate will decline as population density increases (which is clearly false) and to other similarly unlikely assumptions. Looking for the purpose of animal or human characteristics can be an extremely helpful contribution of biology to the study of man, but it is also essential to keep this point of view in perspective and to realize that animals are not designed perfectly.

A consideration of specific works by ethologists will demonstrate some of the difficulties of generalizing from animals to man. Desmond Morris's *The Naked Ape* is one of the most popular books of this sort and also in my opinion the worst example. In his introduction Morris states his position clearly: "I am a zoologist and the Naked Ape is an animal. He is therefore fair game for my pen and I refuse to avoid him any longer simply because some of his behavior patterns are rather complex and impressive." To which it would have been appropriate to add, "or because I have never studied him myself or even read very extensively those who have." Morris feels that because he has worked in a zoo and done some research with other animals he is an expert on humans. This is like an electrician who worked on television and radio writing a book on computers. Morris may be qualified to write about other animals and possibly to make a few minor speculations about humans, but he is clearly not an expert and not qualified to say anything as a scientist about human beings. Although Morris's lack of expertise appears throughout the book, he writes very cleverly, and unless the reader pays careful attention he might be taken in.

The basic premise of *The Naked Ape* is that everything that has happened to man is for a purpose. From his initial idea of man as an ape without hair, Morris builds a complicated explanation of why man lost his hair and how this nakedness has led to all sorts of important behavior, including an increase in sexuality and a wide variety of customs. Much of it sounds good at first reading but does not stand up to careful analysis; much more of it seems to be put in to make a case and is simply wrong.

First, to dispose of some minor inaccuracies, Morris's statement that "even the most overstuffed domestic cat demands a nocturnal prowl and the chance to leap on an unsuspecting bird" sounds cute, but tens of thousands of cat owners would deny it. Most domestic cats raised entirely within the house not only would be uninterested in a nocturnal prowl but would probably be terrified of the possibility. Morris states that the act of killing (for the big cats and hunting wolves) has become a goal in itself, a consummatory act. This is a very important point if true, but there is no evidence for it. In fact, Lorenz has argued the opposite, saying that predators kill only for food and do not seem to get any particular joy out of the fight itself.

In discussing the difficulty that early *Homo sapiens* had in surviving, Morris says, "His physique was hopelessly inadequate for arduous endurance tests and for lightning sprints." Now it is true that human beings are not as fast as many other animals in a sprint. The fastest human can run a hundred yards in something under ten seconds (the fastest is 9.0 seconds), which is a little over twenty miles an hour. Any wolf or cat can run much faster than that, and even large animals such as bears and lions can sprint short distances at speeds above thirty miles an hour. Clearly man is not a lightning sprinter. But he does have great endurance. While the fastest time for a mile is a little under four minutes, marathon runners cover twenty-six miles at an average speed of just over five minutes a mile. In other words, Morris is wrong—man may be poor at sprinting but he has remarkable endurance. Minor inaccuracies such as these—which a scientist tries to avoid—creep in unless a writer is an expert in the field in which he is writing.

In the next sentence Morris says that man was "no doubt poor on planning and concentration." This comes absolutely from nowhere. Who knows whether early man was good or bad at planning or concentration? Surely it is likely that compared to every other animal in the world he was extremely good at planning because he was so much smarter.

So much for minor comments—now to examine Morris's main line of argumentation. It is in his discussion of human sexual behavior that he makes his most outrageous statements and most clearly shows the danger faced by someone in one field trying to draw conclusions in another.

Morris's basic notion is that the pair bond is the primary characteristic of human society. He argues that, in a sense, society as it exists today was based on the urge toward pair-bonding, and furthermore, that man's strong sexual urges developed *in order* to maintain this tendency. That is, sexual impulses (and here Morris demonstrates that proclivity for seeking purposes) have the function of keeping pairs together. Sex is the drive that maintains those pairs.

This is quite a notion. It is not what most biologists or sociologists would have said. On the contrary, they would argue that man's strong sexual urges are divisive forces that work against *permanent* pair-bonding. Humans certainly have strong sexual drives that play an important role in their lives. That is one reason why people are gregarious and live together in the first place. But surely these drives generally run counter to permanent pairs rather than supporting them.

Having offered this implausible idea, Morris goes about supporting it. To begin with, he decides that he will base his picture of "normal" modern sexual behavior entirely on North American adults. In this day of internationalism, when it is recognized that no one culture represents the mainstream of human life and that customs vary greatly from one society to another, Morris can still make the statement that "the small backward and unsuccessful societies can largely be ignored. They may have fascinating and bizarre sexual customs but biologically speaking they no longer represent the mainstream of evolution." He thus dismisses 850 million Chinese, 500 million Indians, the continents of South America and Africa, as well as Soviet Russia and all of Europe. North American sexual customs have much in common with those of other societies, but surely it is well known by now that customs in North America differ substantially from those in many other societies both large and small.

Even accepting this selection of North America as the prototype of the *Homo sapiens* in the modern world, it is reasonable to require that the description of North American customs be as accurate as possible. Sadly, this is not the case. To take a particularly dramatic example, Morris seems unaware that there is a high rate of divorce in the United States. He argues time and again that the biological instinct toward pair-bonding is so tremendously strong that it overrides most of the conflicts and cross-pressures in modern society. When he states that this pressure toward pair-bonding is *the* basic drive in human relations and that modern society is largely built upon it, he supports his claim by saying that pair bonds rarely break down. And to support that, he says that the rate of divorce in America was 0.9 per cent (9 out of 1000) in 1956. Whether his figure is a misprint or a misconception, it is wrong. The divorce rate in 1956 was actually 25 per cent (that is, 250 out of 1000 marriages) and has been rising steadily. In the late 1960s and early 1970s it passed 30 per cent, and in some communities it is actually higher than 50 per cent. This kind of error is inexcusable, particularly since the correct figures run so counter to Morris's argument. Since he says that humans are extremely sexual as a means of producing a strong pair bond and keeping the bond together, a key element in his argument is that despite all of the pressures in modern society pair bonds rarely break down. This is clearly not the case at all—at least in Morris's prototypical society of North America. When over 30 per cent of marriages end in divorce (and of course many people who do not get legally divorced are either separated or living together unhappily), it is hard to argue that the biological urges are overcoming modern pressures. In fact, it is even hard to argue that there is a very strong biological tendency toward pair-bonding.

A much more plausible argument is that human beings are quite sexual and that permanent pair-bonding runs counter to this sexuality. Permanent pair-bonding, rather than being a biological tendency, is probably something that society has imposed to counter the normal biological urge to seek diverse sexual partners. Morris says that human beings' very high level of sexuality was developed to keep the pair together, whereas it is more plausible to say that the permanent pair bond developed despite strong sexuality and that it must constantly fight these strong sexual feelings. The difference is extremely important because Morris thinks of both sexuality and pair-bonding as the most basic biological impulses. While sexuality may be a basic impulse, permanent pair-bonding, in the view of most psychologists, is something imposed by society, which is constantly fighting the biological urge. This latter view would explain the extremely high rate of divorce: as the traditional social pressures toward pair-bonding have declined in recent years, the biological urge has again become relatively more important.

Some of Morris's statements about promiscuity indicate a remarkable degree of naïveté. For example, after pointing out that some people were afraid that the widespread use of contraceptives would lead to random promiscuity, he rejects the idea that once fear of pregnancy is removed as a reason for not having sexual intercourse, people are more likely to indulge in it. He says, "but this is most unlikely—the powerful pair-formation tendency of the species will see to that." One wonders at his notions of North American sexual behavior. He seems unaware that most men and women have sexual intercourse with quite a few other people during their lifetimes, many in fairly casual encounters.

Morris even suggests that the existence of the hymen in female *Homo sapiens* is a way of preventing promiscuity, on the grounds that the pain of breaking the hymen is a serious consideration for the female and that she will not be willing to undergo it until "an involvement strong enough to take the initial physical discomfort in its stride" develops. He states quite accurately that "if young females were to go so far (having intercourse) without pair-formation they might very well find themselves pregnant and heading straight towards a parental situation with no partner to accompany them." The hymen, according to Morris, prevents this. It may be that the pain of breaking the hymen is a deterrent to sexual intercourse, but it is clearly not a very effective one, considering the vast number of illegitimate pregnancies that occur in North America—and considering that, as Morris himself points out, a high percentage of women engage in sexual intercourse before marriage, very often with someone other than the person they eventually marry.

What function the hymen performed in the evolutionary scheme of things is unknown. It may serve some purpose in reducing the possibility of disease, protecting the very sensitive and susceptible part of the system, or even conceivably performing the function that Morris attributes to it. It should be clear, by now, however, that it is not serving the latter function very well, and it therefore becomes somewhat foolish to describe it as Morris does as an important element in controlling sexual behavior.

This sampling of the errors and implausibilities in *The Naked Ape* is sufficient to demonstrate the inaccuracies that result when glib generalizations are made from animal to human behavior, particularly when they are based on limited knowledge of the latter.

Robert Ardrey's *Territorial Imperative*, an ethological book more closely related to crowding, popularized the idea that man is a territorial animal with an instinctive urge to hold and defend territory. To support this important thesis, Ardrey says, "our first research, of course, must be for evidence that he is indeed a territorial animal." He later says, "I believe that our century has presented us with the means to demonstrate that our attachment for property is of an ancient biological order."

Ardrey's evidence for man's territoriality is based largely on the difficulties that the Soviet Union has had with its agricultural program. He argues that the collective farming practiced in Russia has failed because the farmer does not own his own land and is therefore less willing to work hard. This is his proof that man has an instinctive territorial imperative.

This is the worst kind of reasoning. To begin with, the facts are questionable and have clearly been selected so as to support the argument. Even if all of the facts were correct, however, the logic is faulty. It is certainly true that the agricultural program of the United States is more successful than that of Russia. The United States produces both more per acre and more per farmer than the Soviet Union. The United States has surpluses of food while Russia in recent years has had to buy wheat from other countries. And it is also true that farmland in the United States is in the hands of individuals while most of Russia's land is owned by the state and worked collectively. Up to this point Ardrey's facts are accurate.

The crucial assumption in his argument, however, is that American farms are more productive because they are family farms worked by just a few people who own them while Russia's farms are unsuccessful because they are huge and worked collectively by people who do not own the land. In support of this he says that most American farms (nine out of ten) are under five hundred acres and are worked by five people or fewer. This is true, but it tells only part of the story. In fact, American farms have been getting larger every year and the average is now almost five hundred acres, hardly a small family farm. In addition, there has been a very strong trend toward huge farms owned by corporations and worked by people who do not themselves own the land. Ardrey claims that "the American agricultural miracle has been produced by a man and his wife with a helper or two on a pair territory," but that is no longer true. The large corporately owned farms are driving the smaller ones out of business, taking them over, and producing a greater and greater percentage of the crops each year. The farms are not owned by the state, as they are in Russia, but are owned by impersonal, distant corporations. It is highly misleading to suggest that advances in American agriculture in the last few decades are due to hard work by small farmers—they are due almost entirely to the introduction of modern machinery, efficient corporate practices, vast irrigation projects, and the products of research on fertilizers, insecticides, and new kinds of crops. It may well be that someone who works on his own farm is willing to work harder than someone who works for the state or for a corporation, but this is not the major explanation of agricultural success in the United States.

Nor is it fair to conclude that Russian problems are due to the collective farm. Admittedly Soviet agriculture has not been as successful as the Russians had hoped and some of the difficulties may have been caused by the size of the farms. On the other hand, the Chinese Communists have apparently been successful in agriculture, and they too use collective farming. It seems likely that success or failure is due not to ownership of the land or even size of the farm, but rather to factors such as how well managed the farm is, the spirit of the farmers, and the natural productivity of the land. Large collective farms have been successful and have failed, small private farms have been successful and have failed.

So much for the facts (or lack of them). Even if the facts are accepted at face value, the argument does not hold up. To explain the "fact" that collective farming has been a failure and small personal farms are very successful, Ardrey proposes the following argument: (1) collective farms are less successful than privately owned ones; (2) this is due to the fact that men work harder when they own their own farms; (3) this in turn proves that men have innate feelings of territoriality. Each step in this line of reasoning is fraught with peril.

Why are collectives less successful than small private farms? Ardrey assumes it is because men work harder on small farms. That may be—it is not implausible. On the other hand, it may be due to a number of other factors. For example, the collectives may have been poorly planned and poorly run. Since they were a new method of farming, there was less experience with them and a number of errors were probably made. In contrast, the small private farm has been in existence for ages and the farmer is more experienced in knowing how to run it. A second, more psychological, possibility is that the collective farmer has less commitment to and therefore less loyalty to the farm than the private owner. Even if the collective farmer works just as hard (perhaps because he is paid by the amount of work he does), he may do things that interfere with the operation of the farm. Just to name one, he may steal food or supplies whenever he gets a chance. All factories and department stores in the United States are aware of this problem, and it probably occurs on collective farms in Russia as well. In addition, the collective farm requires cooperation among a large number of people, and without any great commitment to the success of the farm the individuals may not always get along terribly well. The success of the kibbutzim in Israel is due in part to the strong commitment that everyone feels and to the resulting degree of cooperation. In other words, even if collective farms are less successful than small private farms (which may not be true to begin with), there are many explanations of this other than the one Ardrey offers.

On the other hand, it is plausible that individuals will work less hard for a collective than they will on their own farm, even if they are rewarded on the collective according to how hard they work. This leads to the next and most crucial step in Ardrey's line of reasoning, that this tendency to work harder on one's own land is due to territoriality. This is extremely farfetched. A more compelling explanation of this phenomenon (always assuming that it is true to begin with), might be in terms of pure self-interest on the part of the farmer. If it is his own farm, everything that he does, every bit of work, every ounce of fertilizer, every hour that he puts in is for his own benefit and no one else's. Most workers on collective farms or corporation-owned farms are paid straight salaries or conceivably are given a percentage of the profits. In the first case, of course, there is little reason for them to overexert themselves; in the second case, even though they will benefit from higher profits, they get only a percentage rather than the whole thing. Bean pickers who are paid by the bushel have great incentive to pick as many bushels of beans as they can. But they have no reason to pick only the best beans, to be careful of the ground and the plants, or to do anything that might benefit the farm other than picking beans. In contrast, someone who owns his own farm obviously derives maximum benefit from his own labor. He need not love the farm or the land or the cows or the corn or anything else in order to have a reason to work hard. Presumably he is working the farm in order to earn a living, and the harder he works the greater his income. It is as simple as that, and no complicated biological explanation is necessary.

I hope this makes clear how misleading this argument is as evidence for the existence of an innate territorial imperative in man. Unfortunately this is the kind of argument and the kind of evidence that is often presented as "proof" of innate biological mechanisms in human beings. Since it is difficult to obtain evidence directly, and since the writer has already convinced himself on the basis of observations of other animals such as beavers or crickets or chimpanzees, he resorts to these weak arguments to support what he firmly believes. Generalizations from animals to humans, as already pointed out, do not constitute definitive evidence about human behavior. For that it is necessary to observe humans, and that will be done in the next few chapters.

CROWDING AND CRIME 5

There is no easy way to get an answer to the question of how crowding affects people. As already pointed out, the neat, clean experimental techniques used on other animals cannot be used on people. In order to answer the question, ingenuity must be used to collect evidence without interfering with peoples' lives.

One approach is to take advantage of the fact that some people live under much higher density conditions than others. People in towns are more crowded than people in rural areas, people in cities are more crowded than people in towns, and some cities and parts of cities are more crowded than others. Knowing this, the researcher can look for relationships between where people live and how they behave. If it is found that people who live under high-density conditions differ from those who live under low-density conditions, it is possible to start making intelligent statements about the effects of density.

All of this is not as easy as it may sound. First it is necessary to obtain measures of density for different parts of the country. Then it must be decided what behaviors are to be examined and to obtain measures of them. Perhaps most important and most difficult, controls must be established for the variations in density that go along with variations in other factors, such as economic level and education. There is a strong tendency for poor people to live in crowded areas. Since the object of inquiry is the effect of density on behavior (not density plus poverty), the areas must be equated in terms of income and then examined in relationship with density. Similar controls must be established for other factors, such as occupation, religion, political affiliation, union membership, and color. The ideal situation would be to look at two people who are in every respect identical except that one lives under high-density conditions and the other lives under low. Although this is not strictly possible, the situation can be approximated by various statistical techniques that control for irrelevant factors, permitting assessment of the relationship with density itself.

Most of the research on the effects of density in the real world has dealt with the assumption that crowding causes people to be aggressive. The notion of territoriality is that when people are too close together, it causes an instinctive arousal of aggressive feelings and attack by the person who is crowded. Explanations in terms of adrenal activity also suggest that aggression occurs because of overactive adrenal glands, heightened reactivity to external stimuli, and general nervousness and suspiciousness. As mentioned previously, ethologists such as Lorenz assume that crowding is a cause of violence, as do many sociologists, political scientists, and others concerned with the problem. If crime and juvenile delinquency are regarded as direct effects of aggressiveness, this notion can be tested fairly easily. If crowding does cause increased aggressiveness, more crime and juvenile delinquency should be found in those areas that have a higher population density.

It is easy to understand why people think that crowding causes crime. In the United States there is no question but that more crimes are committed in large cities than in small cities or rural areas. This is hardly a startling finding—practically anyone alive in the United States today could tell you that you are more likely to be robbed in New York than you are in Greenwich, in Los Angeles than in Los Altos Hills, in Philadelphia than in Haverford. Although these observations are based largely on hearsay, for once "common knowledge" happens to be correct. The crime rate per 100,000 people is approximately 1000 crimes per year in rural areas, 2300 in the suburbs, 3400 in small cities, and 5300 in larger cities. The rate of major crimes in the big cities is more than five times as great as in small cities, eight times as great as in the suburbs, and eleven times as great as in rural areas. Crimes, particularly major crimes, occur largely in areas of high population.

But the subject under discussion is the effect of high population density, not large populations. The population of a city is quite a different matter from its density. The largest cities are not necessarily the most crowded, nor do small cities always have low population density. The fact that large cities have more crime than small cities is not a basis for concluding that crime rate is also associated with high density.

Stanley Heshka, Alan Levy, and I conducted a study of the relationship between population density and crime in the metropolitan areas of the United States (see Appendix 1). There are 117 large metropolitan areas that range from New York, with over 7 million, to Charleston, West Virginia, with about 250,000. The densities range from as low as 40 persons per square mile to over 13,000. To begin with, we looked simply at the overall relationship between crime and density. There are areas of high density and high crime but also some with low crime; there are areas of low density and low crime but also some with high crime. Overall, there is a small but appreciable tendency for higher density to go along with higher crime. About 9 per cent of the variation in crime rate is associated with density—not a strong effect, but one that cannot be entirely ignored.

On the other hand, this figure alone means little because density tends to be associated strongly with other factors, such as poverty, educational level, and ethnicity. The crucial question is what happens when these other variables are controlled. The answer is straightforward and unambiguous—when other social factors are equated, the relationship between density and crime disappears entirely. When people's income, education, and other life situations are equal, the level of density under which they live plays no role in the amount of crime they commit.

It could be argued that it is misleading to look at overall crime rates in this context. Stealing a car or robbing a store is not an aggressive act in the usual sense of the word. Ordinarily, people who commit such crimes do not want to hurt anyone but are acting either for money or for thrills. Accordingly, if density does cause increased aggressive feelings, the effect should be relatively slight on crimes of this kind. In contrast, murder, rape, and aggravated assault are clearly directed at persons and generally indicate strong aggressive feelings. Thus, if high density causes an increase in aggressive feelings, this should have a much greater effect on crimes of violence against persons than it should on crimes against property, such as car theft and burglary. Overall crime rates might conceal this important distinction.

The results are exactly the opposite. Even with nothing controlled, the relationship between density and the crimes of violence—murder, rape and aggravated assault—are even lower than with the overall crime rate or crimes against property. Those crimes most related to aggressive feelings, which should be the best indication of the effects of crowding, show absolutely no relationship to population density.

Our results are almost identical with those reported in two other studies of this problem. Pressman and Carol, in a study of metropolitan areas in the United States, found no relationship between density and pathology. In an extensive, careful study, Galle, McCarthy, and Gove investigated the relationship between density and pathology in American cities (rather than the somewhat larger and perhaps ambiguous metropolitan areas), plotting density per acre and household crowding against alcoholism, suicide, and homicide as three examples of pathology. With factors such as education, ethnicity, and unemployment controlled, they found no negative relationships between density or household crowding and any of the three measures of pathology. There were no reliable relationships of any kind between household crowding and pathology, and density per acre was actually seen to have a reverse relationship with suicide and homicide—the higher the density, the lower the rate of these two measures of pathology. Although this reverse effect may be doubted, it is clear that once again density is shown not to be a factor producing pathology in people. Even though major violent crimes are much more prevalent in big cities than elsewhere, this effect cannot be attributed to the higher densities in the larger cities. There is no reason to believe that the density of a community is a factor leading to crime or other pathology.

Despite this lack of relationship between the population density and amount of crime in a city, the true believer in the negative effects of crowding may not be convinced. He could argue that it is unfair to compare one city with another on this kind of variable. Cities differ in so many ways that they may not be comparable. New York is on the east coast, has terrible weather, a large downtown area, tall buildings, subways, and an extensive public bus system, while Los Angeles is on the west coast, has beautiful weather, little public transportation, a pervasive system of highways, few tall buildings, lovely beaches, and lots of swimming pools. Just how these or other factors affect crime rate is not clear, but they may make it unrealistic to compare the two cities. The same holds for all the other cities in the United States—each is unique in some way, has a certain combination of climate, ethnic mix, transportation, educational system, and other features which taken together must play a much more important role in producing or reducing crime than population density. Thus, the argument goes, the lack of relationship between density and crime is not very convincing. This is not a strong argument. Cities do differ from one another, but they also have a great deal in common, and if density affects crime, the effect should be evident in a study of several hundred cities. It should also be evident in studies of high-density areas of specific cities.

In studies made in Honolulu in 1957 and 1966, R. C. Schmitt found that density was associated with high crime rates, even when income and educational level were controlled. The density levels are not particularly high in Honolulu—nor for that matter are the crime rates—but this study did find a relationship between the two. It is the only one that did. All other studies on this problem have failed to find any relationship.

Two studies of Chicago found no relationship between density and juvenile delinquency once income and ethnic factors were controlled. H. H. Winsborough equated the Chicago districts on a variety of social variables and found that density was no longer related to measures of any social or physical pathology. O. R. Galle and his associates did the same thing and obtained the same results. To pursue the possibility further, however, they indulged in some statistical manipulations and eventually teased out a weak relationship even after other factors were controlled. There have been a number of criticisms of their statistics, but even if they are totally accepted, the relationship between density and crime is very low.

Alan Levy, Stanley Heshka, and I have completed a study of density in New York City (see Appendix 2). New York is the prototype of the crowded, modern city. It has over 7 million people in an area of 350 square miles for an average population of more than twenty thousand people per square mile. When it is considered that much of the land is taken up by industry and business, that an additional chunk of it is taken up by parks and recreational areas, and that large areas have almost no one living in them, the actual average density is clearly much, much higher. Manhattan Island is, of course, the true central city. Counting every inch of space, regardless of how it is used, there are still more than seventy thousand people per square mile. At that rate, all of the people in the United States would fit easily into the state of Delaware. Thus, New York is the perfect place to study the effects of population density.

New York is also ideal in another respect. Although it has an extremely high average density, it does have a considerable range. Some parts of Manhattan are fantastically crowded while parts of Richmond and Queens have a density as low as most small towns. This means that high- and low-density areas can be compared to see if density does indeed have a substantial effect on the way people behave.

One other aspect of New York makes it an ideal subject for this research. In most communities, only poor people live under crowded conditions. The rich find houses on the outskirts of town or in special neighborhoods that have low densities. In New York a great many people, both rich and poor, live in high-rise buildings. Although their apartments will naturally differ in many respects, the population density of the neighborhood is often as high in wealthy districts as it is in poorer ones. There are poor people living in high-density areas and there are poor people living in low-density areas; the middle class and the rich also live in both high- and low-density areas. Thus effects of density can be compared while controlling for the effect of income.

Two different measures of density were used. First, we considered the number of people living per square mile in the area. This measure deals with such considerations as how many neighbors there are, how many people there are on the streets, and how much pedestrian traffic one is likely to encounter. In a sense it is the most important measure of density, because it is closely related to the whole question of the population explosion. The more people there are on earth, the more there are per square mile. Nothing can change that fact. Living in high-rise apartments may increase the amount of square feet available, but nothing can increase the amount of land.

The second measure of density is the number of people per room in the housing unit. This involves how much space an individual has where he lives. It has nothing to do with the number of people in the neighborhood, but concerns only the size of his house or apartment. It affects the amount of privacy, the amount of doubling up of the use of space, and the interactions within the family. High density of this kind is not necessarily an urban phenomenon. Poor people on farms in Appalachia or in small towns may have tiny houses. Ten people may share a tarpaper shack or an old cabin. This is much less involved with the population explosion than it is with the amount of money available. And it is obviously more closely related to income than is our other measure. Poor people do tend to have smaller apartments than rich people. Not all poor people have crowded apartments, nor do all rich people have spacious ones, but by and large the measure of room density is intimately related to income.

These are the two basic kinds of density—the number of people an individual interacts with in his neighborhood and the amount of space available where he lives. They affect different aspects of life, impose different kinds of limitations and stimulations, and together should give a good indication of how density operates.

Using these two measures of density, we examined the relationship between them and crime rate as measured by juvenile delinquency. The results are the same as those in Chicago. Income level is strongly related to juvenile delinquency. The poorer the neighborhood, the higher the crime rate. But with income level and ethnicity equated, there is no relationship between either measure of population density and juvenile delinquency. There are about as many high-density areas that have low crime rate as there are that have high crime rate; and about as many low density areas have high crime rate as have low crime rate. This holds for population per acre and perhaps even more surprisingly for density in the houses themselves. Living in a crowded neighborhood or crowded apartment is not associated with committing more crimes.

We next looked at just the lower-income areas. We reasoned that most juvenile delinquency occurs among people who live in such areas. One would think that density would be most unpleasant when it was combined with low income. A rich person living under high-density conditions is doing so from choice and has many compensations, but poor people generally do not have that choice, and any negative factors in the environment should be particularly negative for them. Quite startlingly, there is actually a reverse relationship between density and juvenile delinquency in low-income areas—people who live under higher density have a *lower* rate of juvenile delinquency than those who live in low-density areas. Even in low-income areas, density is not associated with crime rates.

Let me give some examples of the neighborhoods involved. One of the most densely populated neighborhoods in New York is the area west of Amsterdam Avenue between 86th and 94th streets. This is a neighborhood containing a variety of houses. There are extremely attractive large apartment houses on Riverside Drive with views of the river and park, available only to the fairly wealthy. There are also some small brownstones which are not generally expensive, and there are a great many large apartment houses that once were fashionable but are now somewhat run-down. It is a well-to-do but not wealthy area, with an average family income of $7000 per year. The annual crime rate in this neighborhood is twenty-three per thousand; that is, out of every thousand boys under the age of eighteen, only twenty-three per year are involved in any kind of juvenile delinquency that comes to the attention of the police. This is an exceedingly low rate.

Just to the east of this neighborhood, between Amsterdam Avenue and Central Park, is an area that also has a number of attractive houses overlooking the park but is generally less affluent than the other neighborhood. The population density is still very high, but 15 per cent lower than in the first area. The average annual income is only $4900 per family, which puts it just above the average for all of Manhattan. Despite the lower population density, the juvenile delinquency rate is fifty-one per thousand, more than twice as high as in the other area. Density matters much less than income level.

Both of those neighborhoods are densely populated and have fairly high income levels. The juvenile delinquency rate is higher in one than in the other, but even fifty-one per thousand is fairly low for New York City. Consider now a neighborhood on the far east side between 99th and 109th streets, overlooking the East River. This is an area of some tall buildings and some smaller ones, mostly somewhat run-down, but the area is not at all what might be called a slum. The population density is about half of that in the other neighborhoods, but the average income per family is only $3400, close to the poverty level. In this neighborhood of relatively low density and low income, the crime rate is 136 per thousand—almost six times as high as in the densely populated, high-income neighborhoods first considered.

Of course, all of Manhattan is quite densely populated. It is therefore only fair to look at parts of the city that have fewer people per acre. A neighborhood in Brooklyn near Fulton and Putnam has a population density less than a third of those we studied in Manhattan. This neighborhood also has a fairly low income level, and the juvenile delinquency rate is 132 per thousand, one of the highest in the city. Another neighborhood, with a slightly higher density but still less than half of those found in Manhattan, has a whopping juvenile delinquency rate of 189 per thousand.

There are also, of course, areas that have high density and high crime and those that have low density and low crime. The point is that the density of the neighborhood has little to do with its crime rate. Income, educational level, and ethnic background of the people account for most of the variation in juvenile delinquency rates. People who live in low-income areas commit many more crimes than those who live in high-income areas. But density simply does not make any difference.

It should be emphasized that the crime under consideration is that committed by those who live in the neighborhood. These figures have nothing to do with where the crimes are committed. Often someone living in a poor neighborhood will travel to a wealthier neighborhood to commit the crime. The concern here is only with the neighborhood of the person who committed the crime. If high density causes aggressive feelings, there should have been more crime committed by those who lived in high-density areas. There are not and therefore it seems highly likely that population density is not related to crime rate.

Now consider our surprising discovery that there is actually somewhat less juvenile delinquency in low-income areas that have high density than in those that have low density. Even for someone who does not believe that crowding has negative effects, at first glance this is a startling finding. Yet there are a few specialists in urban affairs who would not be surprised at all. Jane

Jacobs, for example, in *The Death and Life of Great American Cities*, argues convincingly that a healthy city or neighborhood is one that has a lot of people in the streets. When there are people on the street, children can be watched by adults, children watch each other, adults watch each other, and everyone supervises everyone else. There are people to talk to, people to interact with, people to argue with, and people to help out if help is needed. When there are a lot of people around, there is activity, vitality and life; when there is no one on the streets, the city is dead. Although the people on the streets may fight with each other and get into some trouble, most of the time nothing serious will happen. Most important, criminals will be frightened off. Why should a mugger attack someone on a crowded street, when he can pick on someone who is alone? The other people may or may not come to the aid of a victim, but why take the chance? Just as a pack of wolves single out the lone deer to attack while avoiding the main herd, criminals tend to pick on people who are alone. In addition, the vitality and activity of the street usually means that people know each other and are more likely to give help when it is needed. The neighborhood is lively, friendly, and therefore much safer. Thus, a high density of people on the streets leads to less rather than more crime.

Anyone who lives in New York City knows the truth of this statement. Broadway is a long, dirty, crowded street that runs the full length of Manhattan Island and then up through the Bronx. Between 72nd Street and 140th Street it is lined with all kinds of stores and shops, ranging from large supermarkets and miniature department stores to newspaper stands, cigarette shops, pizza parlors, all-night cafeterias, book stores, bakeries, and other small businesses. Along most of its length it is not particularly pleasant. The all-night cafeterias and food stands attract drunks, prostitutes, dope addicts, and other unsavory characters, and various parts of Broadway are known as centers of the dope trade. In addition to the bad company one finds on Broadway, the street itself tends to be filthy with the refuse of supermarkets, food stands, and the accumulated garbage produced by vast numbers of people.

One block over to the west is West End Avenue, a fine residential street lined with high-priced apartments that are relatively clean and always very quiet. There are few stores, newspaper stands, or food shops, and accordingly there are very few pedestrians. It is an attractive street, the buildings are interesting, the lobbies of the buildings are well kept and nicely decorated, there are trees and awnings and even an occasional view of the Hudson River.

Two streets—one ugly, dirty, filled with unsavory characters but also with stores and shops and activity, the other attractive, scenic, clean, quiet, and deserted. Where would you feel safer at ten o'clock at night? A stranger to cities might not be sure or might even feel more secure on lovely West End Avenue. But any New Yorker—or for that matter anyone who has lived in cities—will avoid West End Avenue and walk on Broadway if he wants to reach his destination safely. Broadway may be sordid, and all sorts of terrible things may happen within the buildings and down dark alleyways, but on the street itself you are far safer than on West End or for that matter on even more upper-class Park Avenue or Fifth Avenue. As long as there are people around, even not such friendly or pleasant people, you are much better off than when the streets are empty. In the words of Jane Jacobs, busy streets like Broadway "have eyes"—the eyes of shopkeepers, of newspaper dealers, of the people who work in the little bakeries, and of all the pedestrians. The eyes watch and protect. The street is not entirely anonymous. The watchers may not always offer help when it is needed and very few of them will actually rush to your aid if you are attacked, but their presence changes the street from an anonymous, empty passageway to a living thoroughfare; and that change may be the most crucial characteristic of a healthy city.

It is not surprising, therefore, that there is less crime in high-density than in low-density neighborhoods. High density does not cause people to become aggressive, to become muggers or rapists or murderers. It does not cause an increase in criminal activity. On the contrary, it sometimes has the positive effect of making a neighborhood livelier and therefore safer. Note that this does not happen in wealthy high-density areas, because the people stay in their large high-rise apartments and do not venture into the streets. In neighborhoods such as West End Avenue and Park Avenue, the high density does not cause people to be on the streets and does not produce a lively, healthy neighborhood. Because of that, the streets are dangerous and are avoided. When the high density in the neighborhood or in the apartments does produce a high level of activity on the streets, as it usually does in lower-income neighborhoods, there is a corresponding decrease in crime rate.

Whether or not this inverse relationship of high density with crime is accepted as valid, the evidence certainly shows that high density does not increase crime. Cities with high density have no more crime than those with lower density, nor is there a positive correlation between the density of a neighborhood within a city and amount of crime committed by people living there. Although it is always important to keep an open mind and to remember that such research findings are not absolutely conclusive, the evidence available at the moment certainly argues strongly that crowding does not cause crime.

This should hardly be surprising considering what has been happening to both the density and rate of crime in American cities over the past twenty years. The population and density of almost all American cities has remained about constant or has actually decreased during the period. (Manhattan Island, the most crowded area in the country, had a larger population in 1900 than it does today.) But while the density of cities has not increased, the crime rate has skyrocketed. Clearly the increase in crime is not due to an increase in crowding, since that did not occur.

Evidence indicates no effect of density on other types of mental, physical, and social pathology. The studies of Chicago and New York described earlier found that when economic and ethnic factors are controlled, there is little or no relationship between density and such pathologies as mental illness, infant mortality, venereal disease, and adult mortality. People living in high-density areas do not have higher death rates, they do not suffer more from venereal disease or other diseases, they do not enter mental hospitals more often. There is a slight hint that high density might be associated with minor mental disturbances, but the evidence is inconsistent. In general, this research provides no evidence to support the notion that high density is bad for people. There is no consistent or even substantial relationship between the density of a neighborhood, measured either by people per acre or the amount of space in the living quarters, and any pathology.

This conclusion is further supported by the results of a massive study conducted by Robert Mitchell. He was interested in the effect of living space on people's nerves, mental health, and happiness in general. To investigate this he managed to interview thousands of residents of Hong Kong. He carefully measured how much space per person was available in their homes, asked them questions about their health, and conducted various tests of their physical and mental states. Once again, no relationship was found between crowding and health. The levels of density covered a huge range. The larger houses had hundreds of feet per person—as much space as luxury living in the United States. The smaller houses had as little as twenty square feet per person, which is the space available when a family of four lives in a ten-by-eight-foot room. Despite these very high densities, Mitchell found no relationship between crowding and health. When income level was controlled, amount of space had no effect on nervousness, mental health, or expressed happiness. It did, of course, affect how much time was spent in the house and on relationships within the family. As usual, this research shows that amount of space does have effects on how people live, but the effects are not generally negative. A similar study by A. Booth and J. Cowell conducted in Canada produced almost identical results—density had only very small and inconsistent effects on health.

To summarize what has been noted so far about the effects of crowding on people: First, there is no relationship between how crowded a city or neighborhood is and how much crime it has. Although the evidence is not conclusive, it argues strongly that crowding is not causing crime in the cities.

Second, when areas within a city are equated on income, crowded neighborhoods produce no more crime than uncrowded ones. In fact, in lower-income areas, there is actually less crime when there is high density. Poor neighborhoods have more crime than rich ones. Poor people tend to commit more crimes than people with money. Drug addicts commit a high percentage of the serious crimes in the major cities. But there is no evidence that crowding causes crime. Neighborhoods in which houses are close together or where there are many tall apartment buildings, thus producing a high population density, have the same rate of crime as neighborhoods in which the buildings are spaced farther apart or there are fewer tall apartments. Neighborhoods in which there is relatively little space in the apartments themselves, in which people do not have large living quarters, have no more crime than neighborhoods in which the apartments are more spacious. There are a great many reasons why people commit crimes, many factors in modern, complex society that cause crime, but there is no evidence that crowding is one of them.

5 PERSONAL SPACE AND ISOLATION

The previous chapter described some research on the effects of living in cities or parts of cities that have high population densities. It was found that having a great many people per square mile, or even having little space in one's house, has no systematic negative effect on people's behavior. As far as can be seen, it does not lead to any kind of pathology. It does not affect crime or juvenile delinquency or mental illness or infant mortality or any other standard measure of social, physical, and mental pathology.

Although living in a crowded city, neighborhood, or apartment does not seem to have any negative consequences, there is still the possibility that relatively brief exposures to extremely high densities might have substantial effects. A person who lives in Manhattan shares the island with millions of other people, but during most of his twenty-four hours he probably is not exposed to particularly high population densities. His apartment is on the average no more crowded than those of people in other parts of the country; his working conditions may be even more spacious than in most places; and if he drives a car or takes a taxi, there are no more people in the vehicle than there would be anywhere else. During the course of the day he experiences high density more than someone who lives in a small town, but the experiences are relatively short and are generally spread out over the twenty-four hours. He may ride in a very crowded elevator, shop in a crowded store, walk on a crowded street for a few minutes, and perhaps suffer through that most excruciating and most crowded New York experience—the New York subway car. The total amount of time spent under conditions of high density may be less than an hour. Almost every New Yorker is at one time or another exposed to such conditions and therefore can never be unaware that he is living in a very crowded city. Yet his direct experience of high density is limited to these few, relatively short exposures. Therefore, it is important to find out, if possible, how such brief exposures to very intense crowding affect people's behavior and emotions.

Another reason for exploring this problem is that it makes it possible to investigate the effects of crowding more systematically. People obviously cannot be placed in a very crowded room and left there for two or three years. They can, however, be put in a room for a while and observed. In this way the problem can be investigated in the laboratory under controlled conditions and the mechanisms by which high density operates can be probed.

One area of research that is relevant although not directly concerned with crowding is proxemics, the study of personal space. The term was coined by Edward Hall to refer to the study of how people respond to and use the distance between themselves and others. There is no question that the amount of space available and the distance between people is an important element in the environment. It has substantial effects on how someone behaves and also indicates to some extent how he is feeling about the other people who are involved.

Although Hall only made these suggestions, more careful work by Robert Sommer and others has established that people follow quite firmly established rules in how far apart they stand. However, the distance varies considerably depending on several factors, including the relationship between the people and their own personal characteristics. To begin with, the more friendly two people are, the closer they tend to stand. Given plenty of room, friends, spouses, lovers, and parents and children tend to stand much closer than strangers and acquaintances. In addition, a person usually stands closer to someone he likes than to someone he dislikes, even if he knows him equally well. In fact, the distance between people can sometimes serve as a clue to their feelings toward each other. If two people stand quite close to each other at a party (assuming always there is room to move back if they wanted to), it is probable that they like each other and are perhaps interested in each other. "Coming on" to someone sexually often consists in large part of standing closer than usual, thus showing interest without having to say anything directly.

Another factor that affects interpersonal distance is the formality of the relationship and the setting. In a business meeting, people will ordinarily stand farther apart than at a cocktail party, even if they are very friendly. Other things being equal, an employee stands farther from his boss than from someone who has the same job, and if he happens to be friendly with his boss, he will stand farther away at work than in a social setting.

Ethnic groups differ considerably in their preferred distances. Whites in the United States, Canada, and England stand far apart, Europeans stand somewhat closer, and South Americans stand closer still. There is insufficient research to list all nationalities in terms of their interpersonal distances, but these few seem reasonably well established. These differences produce misunderstandings and some awkward scenes. When someone from England meets someone from Mexico, for example, they might execute a complex little dance. The Mexican stands a little closer than the Englishman would like, while the Englishman stands a little farther away than the Mexican considers appropriate. Naturally they cannot both have their way, so they shift back and forth. The Englishman backs up slightly to adjust the distance, the Mexican moves forward to readjust it, the Englishman moves some more, and so on. Eventually, the Englishman may find himself backed into a corner while the Mexican finds that he has been chasing the other all around the room. They both feel misused. The Englishman thinks the Mexican is pushy, aggressive, overly enthusiastic, and familiar. The Mexican thinks the Englishman is cold, distant, unfriendly, and defensive. Yet all that has happened is that they were both trying to stand a comfortable and appropriate (for them) distance apart.

This suggests an important implication: when interpersonal distance is inappropriate, the individual will try to adjust it and will interpret it as having some special meaning. There is no indication that people respond aggressively to someone who stands too close, but they do often feel uncomfortable. The essential point is that the appropriate distance varies according to many factors. Depending on the situation and the initial feeling between the people, any distance from close contact to farther than arm's reach might be "correct." This appears to be true for density as well.

A slightly different consideration involves invasions of a person's space, and this too depends on many factors, one being the relationship between the people involved. If a close friend comes over and sits right next to you in the library, it would not ordinarily be felt as an invasion of your domain, whereas it might be if a stranger did the same thing. If you were not terribly involved in your work and if the stranger were attractive, the "invasion" might be welcome but would still be an intrusion. And if there were no other seats, the act would obviously have less significance. Finally, if the act occurred at a more informal setting such as a cocktail party, it would be significant but would not be considered intrusive.

Research on personal space is important from two points of view. First, it demonstrates that people do respond to variations in the space around them and have rules about what is appropriate. This makes it even more likely that population density affects people's behavior in some way. Second, it shows that there are no absolutes involving this space. There is no "right" distance; there is no automatic negative or aggressive response when someone is close. Instead, the appropriate distance depends almost entirely on such factors as the relationship among the people, the setting, and the personal characteristics of those people. It should not be surprising, therefore, that the effects of crowding are also complex and depend on other factors than the absolute levels of density.

An even more closely related area of research covers the effect of isolation. For many years the United States government has been supporting a series of studies on what happens when people have to live in very small areas for a long time. Interest in this problem has stemmed mainly from the air raid shelter program during the late 1950s and the 1960s, submarine warfare training, and more recently the space program. Before sending people on a three-month space flight to Mars or to live in a space platform for many weeks, it is essential to know something about how they are likely to react.

The basic procedure in all of these studies is to put one or more people in a small room, give them all the food and water they need, and leave them there for an extended period of time. In most experiments the people are given a complicated series of tasks to perform, their physiological and psychological responses are measured, and they are observed through one-way mirrors or closed-circuit television. The amount of space available to them has ranged from very small to fairly large, and the number of days of confinement has ranged from four to twenty.

It was found that most people do well under these circumstances. There are occasional instances of the experiment ending early because the participants could not stand being cooped up any longer, but this was rare. There are few accounts of severe breakdowns, the people do not get into fistfights, no one has been beaten, strangled, murdered, or even slightly mauled. When tasks are provided, they are performed adequately or better. Whatever physiological measures are taken reveal no extreme negative reactions, nor do psychological measures. Although most people probably do not enjoy being isolated in a small space for many days, they can apparently endure these seemingly unpleasant conditions for a long period of time without suffering any ill effects.

In addition to this general result, these isolation studies provide more detailed information on what factors affect people's responses to these crowded conditions. In one experiment, some of the two-man teams were given two rooms so that each member of the team could have total privacy if he wanted it, while the other teams had only one room and therefore no chance for privacy. The nonprivacy condition was also a higher-density situation, since the people had only half as much space and were forced into interactions more often. In other words, a situation in which there was very little space and no chance for privacy was compared with one in which there was twice as much space and the opportunity for privacy. All the odds would seem to be against the first situation: not only is there less space but no privacy. Surely, if territoriality is an important element, if people react badly to crowding, the first situation should produce more negative reactions.

The results of this experiment are somewhat surprising. The small nonprivate condition is not worse—it is better. The men in the smaller room reported that they were less anxious and nervous throughout their confinement than were those who had more room and a chance for privacy. Furthermore, the privacy groups performed their tasks less well.

Another study, by Smith and Haythorn, produced similar results. Groups of either two or three were confined to either very small areas (seventy cubic feet per person) or rooms that were almost three times as large (two hundred cubic feet per person). Neither condition allowed privacy, since all the participants were in one room. Once again, the men in the smaller room coped better. The major measure for the present purpose is the amount of hostility expressed, and there was actually more hostility expressed in the less crowded condition. Whether there were two or three men confined, those in the smaller area got along better.

There are as usual some limitations to this research. In the first place, the participants are not randomly selected from the population. In most of the studies they have been specially selected from one or another branch of the armed services. They are people who are interested in being submarine commanders or want to take part in the space program, or are simply soldiers who volunteer for the research. In other studies they may be civilians, but must necessarily agree to be isolated for long periods of time. This means that those who take part are probably less bothered by isolation and lack of space than the average person. In addition, the participants usually have very high motivation to do well either to prove themselves as a matter of pride or because they actually have something to gain in terms of being accepted into a program or rewarded in some other way. Finally, and perhaps most important, they all know that they will get out of the situation. They know that if it becomes intolerable they can get out immediately. And in any case, after a specified number of days, the experiment will be concluded. Thus, the people involved are somewhat special, their motivation is particularly high, and there is a known time limit.

Despite these limitations, it seems that this research does demonstrate one simple and extremely important fact—people can exist under very crowded conditions for a considerable amount of time without breaking down. There is no getting around this essential finding. This is powerful evidence against the notion that human beings have an instinctive need for territory. If they had this territorial instinct, there should be strong negative effects of this kind of confinement, and they should be more negative (not less) under more crowded conditions, even though they are special people, are highly motivated, and know they can get out if they need to. If the territorial instinct is so weak that it does not appear under these circumstances, then the instinct is not strong enough to be a concern. It seems much more likely that it simply does not exist in human beings.

CROWDING, AGGRESSION, AND SEX

Although it is suggestive, the work on personal space and isolation was not designed primarily to investigate the effects of crowding. Accordingly, most of these studies did not vary the amount of space available and even those that did were not overly concerned about providing proper controls or being sure that they could contrast crowded and uncrowded conditions. Until very recently there was almost no research that focused directly on the effects of crowding on humans. The growing concern with the population explosion and the environment in general has caused a number of psychologists to begin studying the effects of space on human behavior.

A few years ago my friend Paul Ehrlich convinced me that overpopulation was one of the most important problems facing the world, and that everyone who could should do something about it. Paul's best-selling book *The Population Bomb* seems to have had a profound effect on people's consciousness about the problem. I decided that I would do research on the problem of population density, since it was obvious that, despite the efforts of Paul and many others, high density was to be a fact of life for the foreseeable future and it was important to know what effect it had. With a grant from the Ford Foundation and later one from the National Science Foundation, I have conducted a series of studies on the effect of crowding on people. Most of this research has been done in collaboration with my friends and colleagues Alan Levy of Duke University and Stanley Heshka of McMaster University.

We started with the familiar naive assumption that crowding was "a bad thing" and would have negative effects on people's behavior. In particular, we thought that crowding probably was very stressful, would produce tension, and would then produce all the effects that psychologists have found to be associated with high drive. One of the best established effects is that a person who is extremely aroused is unable to perform certain kinds of tasks as well as when he is less aroused. Psychologists have known for years that it is difficult for a person under stress to do complicated jobs, to learn new material, or to think creatively. A familiar example of this phenomenon is a student who is studying anxiously for an exam and finding that he simply cannot learn material as well as he does when he is less nervous. In contrast, some kinds of jobs, especially very simple familiar ones, tend to be unaffected by stress, or in some cases even improved. Athletes typically feel that they have to "get up" for a game, which basically means that they should be extremely aroused and have very high drive. As long as they are not too nervous, this kind of drive seems to improve most kinds of athletic performance rather than interfere with it. Students also experience this phenomenon when they are taking a test and know the material well. They often find that it is helpful to be somewhat nervous, to have somewhat high drive as long as the test is not too complicated. Thus, any particular level of arousal will be ideal for some tasks and less good for others. Whenever arousal is increased, performance will tend to improve on simple tasks and deteriorate on more complex ones. With these findings in mind, we went about studying the effects of crowding by testing people with tasks that were known to be interfered with by high drive and with others that were either unaffected or actually improved under conditions of stress. If, as we supposed, crowding produces stress, it should interfere with performance on the former kinds of tests and improve it on the latter ones.

The first study, conducted with Simon Klevansky and Paul Ehrlich (see Appendix 3) was done in California, and the participants were high-school boys and girls during a lovely summer in the San Francisco Bay area. Groups of students were put in either a large room (200 square feet), a moderate-sized room (120 square feet), or a very small room (about 30 square feet). Since there were nine people in each room, they obviously were either not at all crowded in the large room, slightly crowded in the moderate-sized room, or very crowded in the small room.

A room of thirty square feet is tiny—some closets are bigger. With nine people sitting in the room, everyone had just enough space to put his feet on the floor without touching anyone else's, but there was not an extra square inch available. Each person had something less than four square feet, which is about as little as a sitting human being can occupy. In other words, although this kind of judgment is always subjective, the participants were as crowded as they could possibly be without sitting in each other's laps.

Since we were interested in the effects of crowding by itself, divorced from any other factor in the situation, we did our best to make the rooms identical in all other respects. There was very good air conditioning, which kept all of the rooms at a comfortable temperature. (That is, it did when it worked. One hot August day the air conditioning broke down in one of the rooms and we didn't discover it for several hours. Finally, somebody complained—when the temperature had hit 98°. Imagine that tiny room, full of people, with the temperature hovering just below 100°. Yet, man's adaptability is so remarkable that even under these circumstances there was no indication that the people in that room did any worse than those in any other room.) In addition, there was a very good ventilation system which kept odors at a minimum, there was no smoking, and the floors and walls were insulated enough so that the rooms were about equally noisy. Thus, any differences in performance from room to room must have been due to the degree of density in the rooms rather than to any other variations.

The participants stayed in the rooms three hours a day for three days. During that time, they worked on a variety of tasks that represented a wide range of skills and abilities. Some tasks were extremely simple or even simple-minded—for example, participants were required to cross out all the sevens on a page of random numbers. Another task consisted of memorizing a series of words that were read over a loud speaker. The words were read once, and then the subjects were asked to write down as many as they could recall. Still other tasks required a certain amount of ingenuity and thinking. Subjects were given scrambled letters and told to make a word of them, or they were given a long series of letters and told to make as many different words from them as they could. More complex tasks consisted of being given the name of an object (e.g., brick) and told to think of as many different uses for it as they could. This task has been used as a measure of originality and creativity. Some of these tasks were worked on individually, and some, such as the uses for a brick and the anagrams, were worked on both alone and as a group. We were interested in finding which kinds of tasks would be affected by crowding and which would not.

After running hundreds of subjects for thousands of hours, we discovered that crowding had no effect on performance on any of the tasks. The people in the small room did just as well as those in the middle-sized and large rooms on all of the different tasks. We thought that perhaps the effect of crowding would occur only after some time, so we compared the beginning of the session to the end. But once again there was no effect of crowding on task performance—whether at the beginning or at the end of the session, the small room did not differ appreciably from either of the other rooms. On dull simple tasks, on memory tasks, on tasks requiring concentration, and on tasks requiring a high degree of creativity, crowded subjects did just as well as, and sometimes better than, uncrowded subjects. There was no hint, not the faintest suggestion, that being crowded either interfered with or improved performance. It simply did not have any effect.

Although by now we are all quite convinced that crowding does not have generally negative effects, at the time we were startled. Like almost everyone else who thinks about this problem, we assumed that crowding acted as a stressor and would interfere with performance on complicated tasks. When we failed to find that, the belief was shaken but persisted. Therefore, to be more certain of the results, we repeated the study, this time using different tasks and an entirely different group of subjects. Instead of high-school boys and girls who might be particularly adaptable or more used to conditions of high density, we hired women from a temporary employment service. These women ranged in age from about twenty-five to sixty, had no particular skills although most of them had done some office work, and had a fairly low level of education. As in the first study, they were put in either small or large rooms, sat on comfortable chairs, and worked on tasks for three hours. Also, to make sure that the great variety of tasks that we used before did not in some way interfere with our effect, we gave the women only three different tasks. They crossed out numbers on a sheet of paper for an hour, worked on the brick-uses task for twenty minutes, and spent another hour doing anagrams. They were all quite bored by the work they were doing and throughout tended to treat us as crazy youngsters asking them to do something terribly silly. Nevertheless, they were extremely cooperative and as far as we could tell worked very hard.

When results were in, our previous doubts vanished almost totally. Once again, there was absolutely no effect or even hint of an effect due to the size of the room. The crowded women performed just as well on all of the tasks as those who were less crowded.

Since that time a number of other experimenters have asked people under crowded or uncrowded conditions to perform a variety of tasks. The isolation studies mentioned earlier found no differences in performance as a function of the amount of space available. In addition, a study by W. Griffitt and R. Veitch was not designed to investigate task performance, but did give subjects a task just to fill some time. A personal communication from the authors indicates that there was no difference in performance between crowded and uncrowded subjects.

This work indicates strongly that crowding for the

periods of time studied here and to the degree used here does not affect task performance. More to the point, it suggests that crowding is not a stressor in the usual sense of the word—that it does not arouse people's drives or cause them to be tense or hopped up. Other factors that do arouse drive—for example, the threat of electric shock, pressure to finish a job in a given period of time, or higher incentive for doing well—all do have substantial effects on task performance. But crowding does not and we can now conclude with some confidence that at least under the circumstances studied here, and probably under all circumstances, crowding itself, separate from smell or heat or fear or physical discomfort, does not produce stress.

Anyone who has been reading this book from the beginning will probably not be surprised by this result. After all, there seems to be ample evidence from work on animals, from the work on correlational studies in the cities, and from the isolation studies that crowding is not necessarily a stress-producing condition. Sometimes people seem to respond positively to crowding, sometimes negatively, and often they do not respond one way or the other. It is important to remember, however, that until this work that has been done in the last few years, most people who thought about crowding believed that it was perhaps one of the major sources of stress in modern society. Naturally, once crowding is believed to produce stress, it becomes a negative influence and would be expected to have all sorts of bad effects. On the other hand, the current work, added to what came before, shows that this is not correct. Crowding is thus freed from the label of a simple stressor, and the fact must be faced that it is a much more complicated factor in human life than previously realized. Accordingly, we turned to a series of studies designed to investigate the effects of crowding on more complex social behavior.

As a matter of fact, all of us working on this research decided at this point that it was "obvious" that whatever effects crowding had would be on social behavior. After all, we reasoned, the presence of other people in a small space was a social not a physical phenomenon, and therefore it would be expected to have its main effects on social rather than nonsocial behavior, such as performing a task.

Accordingly we decided to study the effects of crowding on social behavior and concentrated in particular on aggressiveness, for several reasons. First, it is probably the most widely believed effect of crowding. Although research on the relationship between density and crime in the city does not support this idea, it still is widely accepted—and we thought it might apply to short-term crowding, the kind we were studying in the laboratory.

Second, we did believe that crowding might affect the feelings of the participants for one another. If they were crowded together, and if crowding had any effect on social behavior, the effect would be shown in how they felt about one another. Presumably, if there were generally negative effects, they would like each other less under crowded conditions than under uncrowded ones, and this change in liking should be reflected in more aggressive behavior.

Other investigators were doing somewhat similar studies. C. Hutt and M. J. Vaizey observed groups of children in large and small rooms and reported that normal children became more aggressive when there was less space whereas mentally disturbed children did not. P. McGrew watched a class of children in large and in moderately large playgrounds and found a slight indication of more fighting in the smaller area. Although both of these studies used few groups and were not strictly controlled, they suggested that crowding might cause aggression. On the other hand, C. M. Loo, observing young children in groups of four in large and small rooms, reported less aggressiveness in the crowded condition. And in our research group Judy Price, in a carefully controlled study, observed twenty-two different groups of schoolchildren in large and small play areas, with each group being in both size areas so that their behavior under the two conditions could be compared. There was no effect of size of the room on aggressiveness. While the results of these observational studies have been inconsistent, the more extensive and controlled work has found no negative effect of crowding. This body of evidence was one more reason to focus on the possible effects of crowding on aggressiveness and especially on the feelings among the members of the group.

The first study we conducted along these lines (see Appendix 4) was in some ways quite similar to the earlier ones we had done. Groups of high-school boys or high-school girls were put in either a very small or a larger room. In the small room they had about six square feet per person; in the larger room, twenty square feet per person. The four men or women in the group were given a chance to introduce themselves, discuss various problems, and generally get to know each other. Then, after being in the room for several hours, they were asked to play a simple game. The key point of this game, which is called the prisoner's dilemma, is that it can be played either cooperatively or competitively. If all of the members of the group cooperate, they can all win a fair amount of money. We were actually paying them, so a perfectly cooperative group would win four dollars a piece. On the other hand, the people can try to compete with each other. If they do that, there is a chance that any one person can win a lot more money, but the group as a whole is absolutely certain to win less. In addition, any time somebody tries to compete, even if he succeeds on that trial, it means that the other members of the group will lose a lot of money. Thus, it is clear that competing is a selfish and to some extent aggressive strategy, while cooperating is unselfish and unaggressive.

Note that by the time they played this game, the participants had been in the room for several hours. They had interacted in a variety of ways. They talked informally about themselves, discussed controversial topics, and played a simple game. If these interactions aroused feelings of hostility or friendliness, they might be expected to affect the level of cooperation in the final game. Up to this point there were no obvious differences among the groups, but we had not yet taken any measures of feelings within the group or of aggressiveness. The point is that the people did not enter a crowded or uncrowded room and immediately respond. They had several hours to get to know one another and develop feelings about the group.

The groups played this game for twenty trials, and we are mainly interested in how much competition there was in the small and large rooms. First, overall there was no effect of the size of the room. There was just about as much competition in the small room as there was in the large room. Once again, crowding did not have a generally negative effect. However, and this is the surprising and somewhat startling finding, there was a big difference in the reaction of the all-male and all-female groups to crowding. Groups of girls were somewhat less competitive in the small room than they were in the large room. In contrast, groups of boys were more competitive in the small room than they were in the large room. In other words, the girls responded positively to a lack of space by becoming more cooperative, while the boys responded negatively, becoming much less cooperative.

This was certainly baffling. Were we to conclude that men and women differ in their response to space? Or was it due to something special in this particular situation? In order to see whether we could count on this effect, we repeated the study using entirely different subjects and an entirely different situation. This next study (see Appendix 5) was conducted in New York City rather than in suburban Palo Alto. The participants were people who responded to a classified ad in *The New York Times*, ranged in age from eighteen to eighty, and came from a wide variety of ethnic groups, economic backgrounds, and professions. This time groups of all men, all women, or both men and women were placed in a small or large room and were asked to consider themselves a jury listening to a courtroom trial. The groups ranged in size from six to ten, with corresponding densities being about twelve square feet per person in the small room and twenty-five square feet in the large room. We played tape recordings of five very brief trials, and after each one the participants decided on a verdict of guilty or not guilty and also on the severity of sentence if the defendant was guilty. The trials were actually made up by us but sounded authentic. They included a case of arson in which somebody died, a violent rape of a young woman, a purse-snatching in which an old woman was knocked to the ground and badly hurt, a hit-and-run driving accident in which a child was injured, and a strange case of a man who booby-trapped the trunk of his car to prevent robbery and caused severe injury to someone who then opened it. In each case, there were prosecution and defense witnesses, cross-examinations, summations by both lawyers, and a charge to the jury by the judge. All of the cases were designed so that the defendant seemed guilty to most listeners but that there was room for some doubt.

The participants in the study listened to each case and then arrived at a verdict without any discussion. They decided whether the defendant was guilty or not guilty, and if guilty how severe the sentence should be. Thus, unlike a real jury, the decisions were reached individually and were private. There was no possibility of anyone being influenced by anyone else. However, for the last three cases, after these individual decisions were reached, the group discussed the evidence in detail and the participants recorded a second decision privately. There was therefore a considerable amount of interaction among the group members—they expressed opinions, went over the evidence, and generally had quite lively discussions and even arguments.

After giving their verdicts on all five cases, the participants indicated on questionnaires how much they had enjoyed the sessions, how much they liked the other members of the group, and how good a jury they thought they had been. These questions were designed to assess their emotional reactions to the situation and to the other people in their group.

Our first piece of evidence is the severity of the sentences that were given. There is a remarkable similarity between these results and those of the previous experiment. Once again, there is no overall effect of crowding. Taking all groups together, the small room and large room do not differ appreciably in the severity of the sentences they gave out. Crowding had no general negative or positive effect on this behavior. However, there are substantial differences between the all-male, all-female, and mixed-sex groups. Just as before, the groups of women seem to respond positively to crowding, giving less severe sentences in the small than in the large room. In contrast the groups of men respond somewhat negatively, giving slightly more severe sentences in the small room. And the mixed-sex groups seem to be unaffected by the size of the room. The group as a whole gives about the same sentences in the two rooms, and the men alone and the women alone in the mixed-sex groups also do not differ for the two sized rooms.

These results are duplicated almost exactly by the finding from the questionnaire. The all-female groups in the small room report that they like each other more, find the session more pleasant and the people more friendly than those in the large rooms; while the all-male groups have the opposite preference in each case, being more positive in the large than in the small room. And the mixed-sex groups once again do not differ as a function of the size of the room.

Thus, there is a clear, consistent pattern across these two studies. All-male groups respond negatively to crowding, becoming more competitive, somewhat more severe in their sentences, and liking the other members of the group and the whole experience less in a crowded condition. All-female groups respond positively, being less competitive, giving less severe sentences, and liking each other and the session more when they are crowded. When the group is composed of men and women, there is no effect of the size of the room.

In the last few years, several other investigators have also found that men and women responded differently to crowding. M. Ross and his colleagues found the same pattern we did—women being more positive in crowded rooms and men less positive. J. E. Marshall and R. Heslin in an unpublished paper reported almost opposite results—in mixed-sex groups both men and women were more positive when crowded than when uncrowded, while in same-sex groups, men were more positive when crowded while women were less positive.

And, in a study referred to earlier, Loo, using children, also found a pattern diametrically opposed to ours. With mixed-sex groups, girls were unaffected by the size of the room but boys were *less* aggressive in a small than in a large room.

These findings, added to ours, are provocative but confusing. Although they indicate strongly that the effect of density is to some extent dependent on the sex of the group members, there is no consistent pattern to these effects. Sometimes all-male groups respond negatively to high density, sometimes they respond positively, and sometimes density has little effect on their behavior. Similarly, all-female groups show all three responses. And mixed-sex groups sometimes show little response to density, but in other situations the whole group or one of the sexes responds strongly to the amount of space. The work thus demonstrates the complexity of the phenomenon without clarifying the situation. Obviously, what is needed is some overall theory that can account for a wide diversity of effects, and such a theory will be presented in the next chapter.

DENSITY-INTENSITY: A THEORY OF CROWDING

8

It has been shown that population density bears little or no relationship to any kind of pathology among humans. While conditions of high density, either in a neighborhood or within one's own dwelling, obviously have substantial effects on how one lives, they do not appear to have generally negative consequences. Under more controlled circumstances, research demonstrates that people can function quite well even when very crowded and isolated for considerable periods of time. Indeed, at least within the limits used in these studies, increasing the density has, if anything, positive effects—reducing hostility and stress. Density has also been shown to have no effect on performance on a wide variety of tasks, thus making it seem highly unlikely that it produces stress in the usual sense of the word. Most provocatively, a series of studies has found that density sometimes does affect aggressiveness and interpersonal feelings, but that these effects are different for males and females. Furthermore, the direction of the differences is not consistent—males responding negatively to high density in some experiments and positively in others, with females also showing both tendencies. This recent work indicates that crowding can affect interpersonal behavior but that its effects are quite complex, depending on other factors in the situation. Because of the lack of consistency, it seems doubtful that males and females have basically different reactions to density. Rather, a more general principle is necessary to explain all of the diverse results.

I propose that crowding by itself has neither good effects nor bad effects on people but rather *serves to intensify the individual's typical reactions to the situation*. If he ordinarily would find the circumstances pleasant, would enjoy having people around him, would think of the other people as friends, would in a word have a positive reaction to the other people, he will have a more positive reaction under conditions of high density. On the other hand, if ordinarily he would dislike the other people, find it unpleasant having them around, feel aggressive toward them, and in general have a negative reaction to the presence of the other people, he will have a more negative reaction under conditions of high density. And if for some reason he would ordinarily be indifferent to the presence of other people, increasing the density will have little effect one way or the other. Thus, people do not respond to density in a uniform way, they do not find it either always pleasant or always unpleasant. Rather, their response to density depends almost entirely on their response to the situation itself. Density acts primarily to make this response, whatever it is, stronger.

A rough analogy would be the effect of the loudness of music. Turning up the volume on a hi-fi set has many of the same effects on response to the music that increasing density has on response to the presence of other people (assuming that the music is not so loud that it actually causes physical pain). If a person likes the music and is enjoying it, increasing the volume will usually make him enjoy it more. He will hear it better, pay more attention to it, be able to appreciate more of the subtleties and overtones, and generally find the music itself more enjoyable. In contrast, if he dislikes the music, increasing the volume will make him like it even less.

Although the analogy is fairly rough, it helps to understand the notion of how crowding operates. Just as with music, the presence of other people produces responses of various strengths. If there are ten people in a very large room, the impact is different from when the same ten people are in a small room. In a sense the "amplitude" of the stimulus is changed. In the low-density condition, the individual can largely ignore the presence of the other people, they impinge on his consciousness relatively little, he need not interact with them as closely, and in general they are a less important, less pervasive influence. In virtually every way, the individual's interactions with the people in a low-density condition are less intense and less important than in a high-density condition.

This difference between high- and low-density situations is more obvious under some circumstances than others, but it almost always exists. Consider a few examples. Six people riding in a bus will have practically no interactions unless they know each other to begin with. They will sit in separate seats, probably spacing themselves around the bus so that there are even several seats between them. They need not touch each other in any way, talk to each other, meet each other's eyes, or even look at each other very much. The same six people riding in a minibus would have to sit near each other, probably touch occasionally, almost certainly look at each other. They can perhaps still avoid talking, but clearly there is some minimal level of interaction due to the lack of space. And finally, if the same six people share a car, they will be touching throughout the ride, will have to look at each other unless they deliberately avoid it, and there will be strong pressure to interact more directly. It is, of course, possible to share a car with five other people and never interact, but even if the people do not know each other to begin with, the chances are that there will be some social interaction. The physical proximity due to the high density makes the presence of the other people much more important and almost forces some kind of interaction. Furthermore, if the other people are unpleasant in some way—perhaps frightening or obnoxious—being with them should be more unpleasant in a car than in a minibus, which should in turn be more unpleasant than being in the large bus. Whereas if the other people are particularly pleasant, it should be most enjoyable being with them in the car and least enjoyable being in the large bus.

Imagine a cocktail party with thirty people in either a large or small room. When the room is large and the density correspondingly low, the level of interaction tends to be much less intense and intimate. People may be scattered around the room in small clumps, talking to only one or two other people. Although these interactions may be fine, the impact of the party as a whole is relatively slight. There is not the feeling of an exciting, stimulating party. Under these circumstances, if the other people at the party are not particularly pleasant, it is fairly easy to avoid interacting with them; if they are pleasant, it is somewhat more difficult to interact with them than if the room is smaller. Instead of being forced into close proximity where interactions necessarily occur, one must seek out a person to talk to. This does not, of course, prevent interactions, but it does make them somewhat harder and probably more diffuse. Under these circumstances people will usually crowd together in one corner of the room, or as so often happens at parties, in the kitchen. In this way, they increase the density so as to liven up the party.

In the small room with high density, avoiding interactions is virtually impossible. Everyone is in close proximity to everyone else, they find themselves face-to-face with other people, there is a high level of interaction that does not exist in the larger room. If the other people are unpleasant, it is still necessary to interact with them; if they are pleasant, one does not have to make a great effort to interact. This means that the characteristics of the other people are much more important in the small than in the large room.

Once again, this is a familiar experience for most people. Assuming that the people at the party are congenial, it is almost inevitable that the party will be better if there is fairly high density. Parties in large empty rooms are always unexciting and disappointing. In small rooms, as long as it is a good group of people, the party tends to be more successful. In fact, most good hosts and hostesses know that one ingredient in a good party is the right number of people for the size of the room. If it is going to be a stimulating, exciting party, there cannot be too few people relative to the amount of space. Of course, there is some limit to the number of people that can squeeze into a room, but within a broad range, the higher the density, the more exciting and stimulating a party will be.

Obviously, just as with sound, at some point there is such intense crowding that it becomes unpleasant, but even at this level the effect is due primarily to such factors as physical discomfort, odors, and lack of freedom to move. The mere experience of being with many people in a small amount of room is not negative; it only becomes so when it is associated with these other, clearly negative factors—and that occurs only at extremes such as occur in packed subways. Even an extremely crowded party, with very little space available, rarely reaches this level of density. The essential point is that unless this "breakpoint" is reached, density itself is not unpleasant but rather depends on the situation, and operates by intensifying reactions to the other people.

In general, there does seem to be an intuitive feeling that the effect of crowding depends on whether the situation is inherently pleasant or unpleasant. If it is the kind of experience that would ordinarily be fun, in which the interactions among people are usually pleasant, crowding usually has either no effect or actually enhances the enjoyment. On the other hand, if the situation would ordinarily be difficult for one reason or another and the interaction among the people is unpleasant, crowding will usually make things even worse. Sitting in a doctor's waiting room, taking a test in a class, waiting on line at an airport, or traveling in the New York subway are usually unpleasant experiences, and most people would agree that crowding makes them even more unpleasant. In contrast, watching a football game or a play, riding on a cable car in San Francisco, spending a day at an amusement park, and attending a cocktail party are pleasant experiences and for most people are made even more exciting and enjoyable when the density of people is fairly high. Crowding intensifies the normal reaction—making a bad experience worse and a good experience better.

It is important to distinguish between this idea and the two common assumptions that high density produces stress or arousal. Taking these one at a time, there is no evidence that high density is a stressor. Pain, fear, hunger, electric shock, extremely loud noise, and similar kinds of stimulation are stressors. The individual subjected to them clearly finds them unpleasant. He will report that he is anxious and suffering from physical discomfort and will also manifest certain predictable behavior. In particular, he will perform less well on most complex tasks and better on some simple ones. Given a chance, he will escape from the situation.

None of this occurs with high density. There is no evidence that people are especially anxious nor that they are suffering physical discomfort (as long as they have enough room so that they are not actually touching). They do not perform less well on complex tasks, nor better on simple ones. And they do not try to escape from the situation. Indeed, under many circumstances they find the experience more pleasant and are less anxious than people under conditions of lower density. In addition, long-term high density as it exists in the cities is not related to physical or mental breakdown. With other factors controlled, high density is not associated with more illness, higher infant or adult mortality, higher rates of suicide, or mental illness. If high density were a stressor, all or some of these effects would be expected. Neither the hard data nor the subjective reports of individuals exposed to high density support the idea that it produces stress. As long as such factors as heat, space to sit, odors, and poverty are controlled, high density is not a stressful situation within very broad limits. In fact, even among other animals, most of the evidence is that density alone does not lead to physical pathology, and it is therefore probably not stressful for them either.

The notion that high density produces arousal (though not stress) is more complicated. A high-density situation could stimulate a person and get his mind and body more active, without being stressful in the sense of unpleasant. This appears to be true among other animals, at least under some circumstances. Group-reared animals do have enlarged adrenal glands, which is an indication of arousal. However, the evidence on humans does not support this idea. Although simple arousal would not be expected to cause any kind of pathology, it should affect task performance. One of the most solidly established findings in the field of motivation and learning is that arousal facilitates performance on simple tasks and interferes with it on complex ones. Since high density does not affect task performance on either kind of task, it seems unlikely that it acts as an arouser. In addition, subjects do not report feeling more aroused in high-density conditions, nor do any of their responses or other behavior indicate such arousal. At the moment there is no research to support the hypothesis that high density is arousing.

Nevertheless, the possibility remains that high density is arousing under some conditions. The research conducted so far does not rule it out definitively, because only a few experiments have tested it directly. There have as yet been no comprehensive tests of physiological responses to high density. In addition, the failure to find arousal effects might be due to the fact that participants are already quite aroused by being in a psychological experiment, which is unusual and perhaps exciting for most people. Therefore, the mind should be kept open to the idea that high density is arousing but not stressful.

It should be made clear that this theory does not consider high density to affect arousal at all. The density-intensity theory is that crowding increases the importance of the other people in the situation just as a five-dollar bill is more important than a one-dollar bill or a large painting is more important than a small one.

Louder music, brighter light, stronger tastes, bigger pictures are more important stimuli but are not stressors and do not generally increase arousal. Consider a painting on the wall of a room. Under most circumstances, a small painting is less important, attracts less attention, and produces a weaker response than a large painting. A person walking into a room that has two paintings, one two feet square and the other eight feet square, will almost certainly notice the latter first and respond to it more strongly. If he likes it, it will have a more positive effect on him and on the room than if he likes the small painting; if he dislikes them both, the large painting will have a more negative effect than the smaller one. Neither produces stress (unless the person really detests them), nor does either produce arousal in the usual sense of the term. Physiological tests would not find a heart beating faster or an increase in blood pressure because of a large painting (again unless there is some other reason for an unusually strong reaction). Yet, without stress or arousal, the larger painting does produce a stronger response than the smaller one. According to the density-intensity theory, the density of people in a room operates in exactly the same way. Increasing density does not produce stress or arousal, but it does make the presence of the other people and their characteristics more important. An individual will pay more attention to them, and whatever the individual's reactions, they will be stronger.

How does this theory apply to our finding that men respond negatively to crowding and women respond positively? It is likely that for most men in our society, entering a room full of other men in a formal, scientific setting is a somewhat threatening experience. Men typically think of other men as rivals, are suspicious of other men, and in particular are prepared to have to prove themselves or to compete with other men. When they arrive and find all other men in the room, their natural response is one of suspicion, defensiveness, and perhaps even mild hostility. Certainly, their competitive feelings tend to be aroused by a group of other men, particularly when they are then asked to play games or take part in a discussion. Accordingly, the men tend to have a somewhat negative, hostile reaction to the other men in the situation. According to the density-intensity theory, this negative response should be strengthened by high density. Thus, the men would be expected to be somewhat suspicious and hostile in the low-density condition and to become more so when density is increased.

Although there is no good evidence for this speculation, it seems probable that most women in our society have a less competitive and hostile reaction to a group of other women. There are undoubtedly great variations in this, but it does seem as if women compete less with each other (at least openly), are less suspicious of each other, and feel less that they have to prove themselves in the presence of other women than men do with other men. In fact, most women probably respond to a group of other women as a potentially interesting, intimate, friendly group. Therefore, when they enter a room full of other women, their responses are generally somewhat on the positive side, and these responses should be more positive under conditions of high density than under conditions of low density.

Finally, when the sexes are mixed, the situation is much more ambiguous, and neither men nor women have clearly positive or negative responses to the group. Therefore, increasing the density will not make their response either more positive or more negative, since they are mixed to begin with. Probably some subjects have a positive response to a mixed sex group and others have a negative, and therefore increasing the density will not have any overall effect.

One study that showed clearly the opposite pattern was conducted by Loo and involved young children who knew each other. This is quite a different situation. Presumably the general tendency for all of the children was to be friendly. Very little fighting occurred in any condition, and even that was not terribly serious. In these circumstances, increasing the density would be expected to intensify the generally friendly feelings and reduce the amount of aggressiveness. Indeed, that is exactly what happened. The boys, who were the only ones doing any fighting, did less of it when crowded than when not crowded. The girls did no fighting under low density, and increasing the density had no effect. These results can thus be explained in the same terms as the others.

The one result that we cannot explain is that by Marshall and Heslin, who found men more positive when crowded in same-sex or mixed groups, with women being more positive when crowded in a mixed group but more negative when crowded in a same-sex group. This is certainly baffling, since the situation sounds similar to ours and the results are almost exactly opposite. The finding is probably due to specific variation in the circumstances and the people who served as subjects, but we freely admit having no clue as to the critical factors.

Finally, an experiment by Griffitt and Veitch found generally negative effects of high density for all subjects. In this study, people were seated in rooms in such a way that they did not face each other. They were not introduced, did not interact in any way, and merely carried out some individual tasks. It was not a social situation in the usual sense of the word, since there was no interaction. In addition, it was probably fairly unpleasant regardless of condition since the tasks were dull, the seating arrangement unnatural, and the rooms bare and uncomfortable. Under these circumstances, everyone should have a somewhat negative reaction, and increasing the density should, if anything, intensify that response.

Thus, with the exception of the Marshall and Heslin study, all of the results are consistent with the density-intensity theory. The idea that density intensifies the typical social reaction provides a plausible explanation of all the findings. Naturally, since these explanations are offered after the results are obtained, there is no proof they are correct, but it is important that the theory can account for these diverse findings fairly easily.

A series of experiments were designed specifically to test this theory. The theory states that any response to other people—whether positive or negative—should be strengthened by increasing density. Whatever the response is under low density, it should become stronger under high density. Therefore, in order to test the theory, it is necessary to set up a situation in which the social interaction is deliberately made either pleasant or unpleasant, and then to vary the density. Then, for men, women, or mixed-sex groups, the situation that was deliberately made pleasant should be more pleasant under high density, and the unpleasant situation should be more unpleasant. If this occurs regardless of the sex of the participants, it would disprove the idea that there are innate differences in the response of the sexes to crowding, and would strongly support the theory.

In one study (see Appendix 6) participants were told that we were interested in public speaking. Each person in the group would be required to give a short talk, which the rest of the group would then criticize. We provided a short speech so that the participants did not actually have to make up their talk, as we were afraid that some shy members of the group might find the situation very upsetting if they had to come up with a talk themselves. But all they had to do was read over our little speech and then deliver it to the group. No one seemed particularly upset by this, although naturally some gave the talk better than others. The key point of the study was that for half of the groups the criticisms were all supposed to be positive. We told the subjects that we were interested in only constructive criticism, that while they listened they should concentrate on the good aspects of the presentation, should write down only what they thought were the best qualities of the speaker, and should tell him only good things about what he had done. For the other groups, all of the comments were supposed to be negative. We said that we were interested only in finding problems with the speech, that the subjects should write down only what they thought were the weaknesses of the presentation, and that they should tell the speaker only bad things about how he had performed.

Picture the situation. In one case, the speaker was surrounded by a group all of whom were going to say good things to him. No matter what he did, no matter how he faltered, or how nervous he was, all he was going to hear were positive comments. This surely is a positive situation. In particular, the social interactions are all going to be pleasant. In the other situation, the speaker was surrounded by a group all of whom were concentrating on negative aspects of his performance. No matter what he did, no matter how well he performed, no matter how brilliantly he gave his speech, all he was going to hear were negative comments. This certainly is an unpleasant situation, with the social interactions all being negative.

The positive situation and the negative situation were both done in large and small rooms. The participants were either comfortably arranged in a large room or were crowded together in a small room. Thus, there was either a pleasant or an unpleasant social situation under conditions of high and low density. Naturally all of the participants should find the positive situation more pleasant than the negative situation regardless of the size of the room. The key point is that the reactions—whether pleasant or unpleasant—will be more intense in the small rooms than in the large rooms.

This is exactly what happened. Being criticized was, of course, more negative than being praised, and the subjects responded accordingly. In the positive-criticism condition the participants liked giving the ratings more and found the experience more enjoyable and more pleasant than in the negative-criticism condition. This was true regardless of the size of the room.

More important is the effect of room size. First, there was no over-all effect of density. On no measure of attitude toward the other people or the session as a whole did the large and small rooms differ appreciably, nor was there any consistency in the direction of the small differences that did occur. As usual, crowding by itself did not produce any substantial effects.

However, as predicted by our theory, room size did interact with the pleasantness of the experience. There was a consistent pattern, with the participants in the small room giving more positive ratings than those in the large room under the positive conditions. For example, in rating the speeches when only positive comments were given, they were more positive in the high-density condition than in the low-density; when only negative comments were given, they were more negative under high-density conditions. This was true of almost every measure taken—the positive group in the small room was more positive than the positive group in the large room, and the negative group in the small room was more negative than the negative group in the large room. Clearly, increasing density intensified both positive and negative reactions.

It is important to note that this occurred for all-female groups and for mixed-sex groups, although it was somewhat weaker when the sexes were mixed. Remember that in previous studies it was found that all-female groups responded positively to crowding, suggesting that perhaps females have a general tendency to like high-density situations. The present finding in which females respond more positively under high density when the experience is generally positive and more negatively under high density when the experience is generally negative makes it seem unlikely that women have an innate or learned positive response to crowding. It appears rather that both sexes respond in roughly the same way to density, intensifying their reactions to social situation.

Since we did not have all-male groups in this first study, we conducted another experiment in order to demonstrate the effect with groups composed only of men (see Appendix 7). This study was similar to the first one except that we used a slightly different method of making the situation positive or negative. In this case, the groups worked on complicated problems together in either a large or a small room. The problems consisted of transforming one word into another by changing one letter at a time, being certain that each change produced an acceptable English word. For example, *gold* could be changed to *lead* in the order *gold*, *goad*, *load*, *lead*. The group was given fifteen problems of this kind, one at a time, and allowed a minute to solve each. The difficulty was varied, some problems requiring only two to four steps, others five or six.

The key factor was that we arranged the problems so that some groups could solve all or most of them while other groups could solve only a few. This was done by varying the percentage of difficult problems, half of the groups getting all easy ones and half getting seven easy and eight difficult ones. Accordingly, those groups that we wanted to do well solved twelve or thirteen of the problems, while the other groups solved only five to seven. Thus, some of the groups experienced "success" while others experienced "failure." We reasoned that working together and succeeding would be a pleasant, rewarding, and generally positive interaction, while working together and failing would be unpleasant and negative. As before, we expected that either response would be stronger in the small, crowded room than in the larger, uncrowded room.

Sure enough, the results were very similar to the previous ones. First, the crowded groups were actually somewhat more positive overall than the uncrowded ones. Combining the success and failure groups, those in the small rooms tended to like each other more and feel that the other people were friendlier. Although the size of the room did not produce powerful effects, those that did appear indicate that, if anything, higher density made the experience more pleasant.

The important result for the present purpose is that the small room produced stronger responses than the large room. The failure groups in the small room found the experiment more boring, less lively, and generally a worse experience than those in the large room, while the success groups were in all these cases more positive in the small than the large room. There were no appreciable effects in the opposite direction. Thus, as in the first study, increasing the density magnified the effect of success and failure. It did this for all-male groups even though the previous work suggested that men tend to have negative responses to high density. This finding therefore provides further support for the density-intensity theory. It also directly contradicts two alternative ideas—that people generally react negatively to high density (indeed, whatever overall effects of density occurred showed it to be positive rather than negative) and that men and women have qualitatively different responses to density. We have now seen that all-male, all-female and mixed-sex groups all show the intensification effect.

A third study, conducted by Ilene Staff (see Appendix 8), repeated the first one with a few important variations. Once again, people gave short speeches while others made either positive or negative criticisms. However, in half of the conditions, these criticisms were made by the other people in the room while in half they were made by observers in another room. In other words, half of the groups were giving each other positive or negative comments while half received comments only from outsiders. This raises the critical question of whether the intensification effects previously demonstrated are specific to the reactions to the other people in the room or are more general.

According to the theory, the effect should be quite specific. Increasing density makes other people a more important factor in the individual's life space. His responses to them will accordingly be stronger. But density is largely irrelevant to external factors. The people who are watching through a window and rating the individual are no more important just because there is less space in the room. Similarly, the effect of any other external factor such as the weather outside, noise, or a person threatening to deliver electric shocks should be independent of the level of density within the room. The increasing density should magnify responses to the other people in the room but not to external observers. When the pleasantness of the situation depends on interactions within the room (when the subjects are giving positive or negative ratings), the degree of density should intensify the individual's reaction; when the pleasantness is due to external factors (when outsiders are giving ratings), no intensification should occur.

That is exactly what happened. This time with mixed-sex groups only, the results of the original study were repeated and were even stronger. The members of the positive-comment group responded more positively to each other and to the experiment as a whole in the small than in the large room, while the negative comment groups showed the opposite pattern. When comments came from outside the room, no such effects occurred. There were no consistent differences due to room size. Thus, this study reinforces the findings of the previous ones and also provides the first evidence that the effect is limited to the group itself—reactions to external people are not intensified just because the individuals are crowded.

Our research on the effects of crowding on humans leads us to two conclusions which we hold with some confidence. First, high density does not generally have negative effects on people. This is based on the following pieces of evidence:

1. In the real world, there is no relationship between

crowding and pathology. With income and other factors controlled, cities and neighborhoods that have many people per square mile have no higher rates of crime, illness, infant mortality, venereal disease, suicide, mental illness, or any other pathology than comparable areas with relatively few people per square mile. Similarly, cities and neighborhoods in which the people have little space in their houses or apartments have no more pathology than those in which people have more space. If crowding had generally negative effects, surely they would show up in this kind of survey.

2. People who are put in very small rooms and isolated from the world for periods up to twenty days manage to function quite well. The recent use of the space lab demonstrates that three men can live cooped up in a tiny vehicle performing complex tasks and get along with each other for months. In addition, the few studies in which density was varied actually found less hostility when there was less space. Although all of these studies, as well as the space program, involved unusual circumstances and participants, they certainly indicate that humans are able to cope with high density. Once again, if there were any innate or generally negative reaction to high density, it would be expected to show up in some way in this work.

3. Controlled experiments in which density is explicitly varied have not found negative effects of high density. With one exception, those studies that did find overall effects of density found people responding more positively under high than low density. More important, most experiments have not produced any overall effects of density. There is no evidence from this body of work that crowding causes either stress or arousal. It does not affect task performance, it does not make people more anxious or nervous, and it certainly does not make the experience more unpleasant. If density does have generally negative effects, they should have appeared in these careful experiments.

Therefore, it appears reasonably safe to conclude that high density does not have a generally negative effect on humans. Neither long-term exposure to vast numbers of people in a small space (cities), nor lives spent in cramped and crowded dwellings, nor short-term exposure to very high levels of density in space platforms, isolation chambers, or experimental laboratories causes people to respond negatively. Humans show no hint of territoriality in the sense of reacting aggressively to a lack of space. People will naturally do their best to defend their property from incursions, whether the property be a home, a country, or even a seat on a bus, but they show no hint of territoriality in the sense of an instinctive aggressive response to a lack of space. Whatever the effects on other animals, humans simply do not react negatively to high density per se.

Our second conclusion concerning the effects of crowding on humans is that high density makes other people a more important stimulus and thereby intensifies the typical reaction to them. Experiments have shown complex effects of density. Sometimes males respond negatively while females respond positively, but sometimes the opposite pattern prevails; sometimes both sexes show the same response. My associates and I designed our recent experiments to show that whatever the interpersonal situation, higher density will cause the individual's reaction to be stronger. We showed that positive situations elicited more positive reactions under high than low density, while negative situations produced more negative reactions under high density. This finding can also account for most of the seeming inconsistencies of earlier findings.

A great deal more research, writing, and discussion is necessary to be certain of these conclusions. There are many serious investigators who still need to be convinced, and of course, the common lore that crowding is bad will take a long time to change. But I feel that the evidence is now very strong on the first point and reasonably powerful on the second. While some changes will undoubtedly occur in our understanding of how density affects humans, I think that the two conclusions presented here will turn out to be substantially correct. Crowding is not generally negative and it does intensify reactions to other people.

IN PRAISE OF CITIES

My view of the effects of crowding is obviously optimistic. In contrast, many social critics, social scientists, and ethologists take a pretty dim view, as well they should if their theories are correct. If man does have a territorial instinct or for any reason has an inherent negative response to high density, mankind is in trouble and it is going to get worse. There is simply no ignoring the fact that the world is crowded. There are 4 billion people on earth, and that number is increasing rapidly. Unless there is a major catastrophe or some other dramatic change, the population will double in the next thirty or thirty-five years. Even if the birth rate begins to decline sharply, the population will continue to grow because of the extremely large number of women of child-bearing age. The birth rate in the United States has dropped to the point at which the population should eventually stabilize, but even so the population will probably increase by almost 50 per cent in the next thirty-five years. And there is no indication that birth rates are dropping sharply in the rest of the world. There is the grisly possibility that severe famines in India and Africa will hold the population down somewhat, but barring a nuclear war, a new strain of bubonic plague, or some virus brought back from Mars, it is virtually certain that there will be at least 3 billion more people occupying the earth by 2000 than there are today.

In addition, unless society changes entirely and reverses the trends of the last five or ten thousand years, much of this population will be concentrated in urban centers. Even if the population of the world were suddenly decreased substantially, these high concentrations of people would still exist.

If high population density has negative effects on people, humanity has some pretty rough years to look forward to. In particular, if high density produces aggressiveness which in turn leads to criminality and other antisocial behavior, the world should become a more and more dangerous place to live. Indeed, given the fantastically high densities under which much of the world lives today, it is hard to understand how mankind survives at all.

The density-intensity theory as to how crowding affects people is in marked contrast to this apocalyptic view. I believe that crowding is not necessarily bad and I think the evidence supports this. Although there are many examples of high-density communities that are in serious trouble, there are many that are thriving. As described in chapter 5, there is no relationship between population density and crime rate in the United States. New York City has high density and a high crime rate, but Los Angeles has low density and high crime and there are cities with high density and low crime as well as low density and low crime.

This lack of relationship between density and the health of a city is even more apparent in other parts of the world. The health, vitality, and low crime rate in Holland, Belgium, and indeed most of Western Europe are unaffected by high density. Tokyo, a vast city with very high density, has a fantastically low rate of crime and is one of the most prosperous cities in the world. It is fortunate that the ethologists are wrong about crowding—it does not have generally negative effects on humans. People living under crowded conditions do not become more and more aggressive until they burst. It may be that the theory of crowding as an intensifier will turn out to be incorrect, but it seems almost certain that crowding will not be shown to have strongly negative effects on human beings.

The cities of the world are not doomed. They are not necessarily condemned to high crime rates, riots, and violence. As the population of the world increases, there will not necessarily be an increase in aggressiveness and antisocial behavior and a general breakdown in society. *Homo sapiens* is not doomed to extinction because of population density; the race will not destroy itself simply because it will be crowded. There is some hope for the cities and for mankind—if, instead of taking a fatalistic view or concentrating entirely on problems of population, the world turns its attention to the problems that something can be done about.

This is not to deny that overpopulation and high density cause problems: the increase in population is one of the most serious problems facing the world today. It puts enormous pressures on world resources of food, transportation, housing, energy, and the capacity to handle pollution. We are literally consuming the world we live on without replacing it. We are consuming oil, coal, iron, and other natural resources which simply cannot be replaced. And we are dumping our waste products into the air, land, and seas—giving them more garbage than they can handle and certain kinds of garbage (such as mercury) which they have no capacity to handle. Inevitably, inexorably, they are getting to the point where they will eventually no longer provide us with what we need. This is a direct result of overpopulation and industrialization. Something can be done, such as controlling population, minimizing pollution, and treating waste. It is obvious that not enough is being done, but complaining that population *density* is destroying the world is simply diverting energy from other, real problems.

If it is accepted that population density is not necessarily bad but rather intensifies the social situation, what does this indicate for the urban problem? It certainly indicates that moving people out of the cities is not the answer, except possibly for some communities that simply cannot support the number of people living in them. But by and large the cities are not suffering because of their high density. Most of the major urban centers in the United States have not increased in population (nor, of course, in population density) in the last twenty years and have in fact been decreasing in the last ten. Although the crime rate in New York twenty years ago was extremely low by today's standards, its density then was the same as it is now, and the same is true of many other cities.

It is not density that is producing crime, and reducing density by moving people out of the city will not solve the crime problem. It would reduce the congestion on the streets, make transportation easier, relieve some of the pressure on services such as garbage collection, hospitals, and schools, but people will still require all of those services and moving the people will simply shift the burden from one place to another.

Personally I would hate to see all of the people in the United States scattered evenly over the available land. That would mean that there would no longer be any open spaces or any variations in the kinds of communities available for people to live in. Furthermore, it simply is not feasible; parts of the country are not inhabitable, parts of it are necessary for agriculture, and parts of it are so inconvenient that it would be a great hardship to live there.

The 30 million or so people living in the area stretching from Washington, D.C., to Boston are currently distributed quite unevenly. New York City has almost 8 million and a very high population density, Philadelphia has 2 million, Washington 750,000, and Boston 650,000—all with quite high densities. The surrounding suburbs range from fairly high densities in White Plains and Yonkers to very low densities in the wealthy communities such as Chevy Chase, Wellesley, Westchester, and Oyster Bay. If these 30 million people were distributed evenly over the existing communities, the total density of the area would naturally stay the same, but instead of having peaks and valleys it would even out at a fairly low density. This would eliminate the urban centers, and would dramatically change the whole social and economic structure of the area. Naturally there is no likelihood that such a redistribution would occur in the foreseeable future, but the question is whether a trend in this direction is desirable.

There are at least two reasons—esthetic and economic—why it would not be. First the esthetic. At the moment, each kind of community has a certain positive appeal. New York and the other cities have an excitement, a vitality, a variety that can only be achieved with high population density. These cities are not lovely to look at, they are certainly not always pleasant to walk around, but they do stimulate, amuse, and entertain. The Empire State Building is a beautiful, impressive structure, and the view from its top is breathtaking. Looking down on New York from a high building is a positive esthetic experience, and a walk through Central Park on a crowded Sunday afternoon is both stimulating and fascinating. In contrast, Scarsdale, Oyster Bay, and other low-density suburbs are lovely. Their beautiful homes, trees, gardens, lawns, and open spaces are pleasing to those who live there and to those who have the opportunity to drive through.

For those who can afford Scarsdale or Park Avenue, the existence of both provides a choice. Not everyone who can afford to live in Scarsdale moves out of the city, and not everyone who can afford to live on Park Avenue stays in the city. Even for the less affluent there is a choice between living in the central city, living on the outskirts, or living in the suburbs. The alternatives may not be as pleasant as those offered to the wealthy, but there are alternatives.

If the present uneven distribution were to be replaced by the homogenization of densities, every community would have the population density, and presumably the quality, of a moderately dense suburb such as Levittown. This particular level of density and this particular kind of living are fine for those who prefer them, but the loss of both the excitement of the city and the spaciousness and calm of the suburbs would clearly be an undesirable result.

The second point is largely economic. It requires a high concentration of people to support certain kinds of enterprises that the world would be poorer without. Active, successful theater, for example, can exist only in a densely populated area. Although people from out of town help support it, the theater depends on a concentrated population for a very high percentage of its audience. It also requires services that can economically be located only where there are a large number of theaters, such as a large population of actors and actresses, designers, directors, choreographers, and the other people on whom theater depends. Partly because of this necessity for a very high concentration of people, only the largest cities—either in the United States or in other countries—manage to have a theater season.

The same requirements—although to a lesser extent—hold for opera, ballet, music, and professional athletic teams. The same is true of museums, art galleries, and the production of movies and television programs.

This is also true of fine restaurants—and even not so fine ones—and all sorts of specialty shops. The more specialized a shop, the less likely it is to survive without a high concentration of people. If only one in a thousand people might want to buy a particular kind of product in a given year, only a large city can support a shop that sells just that kind of product. One might ask who needs such specialization, but it provides the kind of enrichment of life that cannot be obtained in any other way.

The variety is also important from a purely economic point of view. It allows and encourages the birth and growth of new businesses. Someone who has an idea for starting a new enterprise must have around him the necessary tools, equipment, and expertise. In *The Economy of Cities,* for example, Jane Jacobs describes how a physicist about to engage in research for an organization outside of New York City came to New York because it was almost impossible to find the supplies he needed anywhere except a major city. She quotes the physicist's shopping list:

From an electronics supply store: one voltage reference diode, five precision resistors of three different sizes, ten alligator clips, one ordinary resistor, a published collection of electronic circuits, a quantity of insulated copper wire, a dry cell, a small potentiometer.

From a store selling surplus electronics equipment: two precision resistors of still other sizes, and a double-pole, double-throw switch.

From a laboratory supplier: a quantity of aluminum sulphate, a specimen jar for crystal growing, glass rod, glass capillary tubing, vacuum grease, epoxy glue.

From a surplus tool store: a screw-threading die.

From a hardware store: two drill bits, a quantity of braided steel wire, silicone sealing cement, screw eyes, two dry cells.

From another hardware store: brass bolts and turnbuckles.

From an industrial hardware store: a drill bit, a hacksaw blade, two fine-threaded large steel bolts and a stainless-steel machinist's rule.

From a plastics supply house: plexiglass sheets of two different thicknesses.

From the factory of a small manufacturer of specialty wire: a two-foot length of extra-fine stainless-steel wire.

From a machine shop: a soft-iron cone, made to order.

From a scientific supply house: two first-surface mirrors and a special lens.

From an aircraft supply house: rubber O rings of three sizes.

There are many places in the country where some of these products could be found, but very few where all of them would be available. Instead of traveling miles in every direction or ordering products by phone, the physicist was able to buy all except the last two within a space of a few blocks in lower Manhattan. The last two items were ordered from suppliers outside of New York and it took him more than twice as long to get them as it did all of the others put together.

The importance of having diverse resources available is probably even more important when it comes to the availability of trained people. This is obvious in the case of entertainment and the arts, but it applies in other areas as well. An expert welder, machinist, artist, letterer, psychologist, writer, or virtually any other trained professional is much more likely to be found in a major city than in an area of lower population density. This does not mean that it is impossible to build a new industry in a low-density area, but it is more feasible to do it where people are concentrated.

For all of these reasons, it would be a great misfortune for the cities to decline in population, for any government agency to encourage a decrease in the concentration of people in the cities, or for anyone to think that the solution to society's problems lies even in part in depopulating the urban centers. On the contrary, the great vitality of the cities is one of the most important resources any country has, and once it is lost it is almost certain that industry, culture, and life in general will begin to decline.

Although some problems obviously are more serious in cities than elsewhere, many are easier to solve where people are concentrated. Often the problems seem greater in cities only because more attention is focused there or because they are more dramatic there. Let us consider very briefly some of the other problems that are supposedly caused by urban living.

Pollution. There is no question but that the air and water around cities tends to be badly polluted. The human, industrial, and automotive waste produced by millions of people and heavy concentrations of industry cannot be easily absorbed by the environment. A few hundred people living in the wilderness produce so little waste that the natural processes of the rivers prevent pollution. A few cars driving through Montana produce just as much exhaust as the same number of cars in New York, but it is easily dissipated in the air. In contrast, even vast Lake Erie could not absorb the waste from Chicago and the other major cities which surround it.

To some extent then, pollution is a much more serious problem in the cities than in less densely populated areas. The greater the population, the more likely it is that the available water and air will be unable to handle the waste products. However, any sizable community faces this problem. Small towns threaten their streams just as surely as large cities threaten rivers. More to the point, a series of small towns along a river pollute it just as much as the same number of people concentrated in a city. In other words, it is the total population in an area that causes the pollution—not the particular distribution. Of course, if the total population were spread evenly over the country, pollution would be less serious in any one place than it is now, but a realistic approach is to compare high-density cities with low-density communities such as other cities, towns, suburbs, and villages—not to rural conditions which constitute only a tiny percentage of American life.

When such a comparison is made, the cities do not appear to be in such bad shape. Every town and suburb now faces the problem of pollution. The air is as bad in the valleys outside Los Angeles as in the city itself; it is worse in Pomona than in Santa Monica; it is as bad on Long Island as in Manhattan. And Lake Erie has been destroyed just as much by all the small towns as by the larger cities. Throughout the country, small streams, lakes, and rivers have been polluted by small communities just as they have been by large cities. Furthermore, it is obvious that a high-density city such as New York or San Francisco presents no less a problem than a low-density one such as Los Angeles—whether the people are spread out or concentrated, something must be done with their waste. Thus, the problem is not really aggravated by high density, and the question becomes whether the solutions are harder or easier.

It seems clear that, at least theoretically (i.e., politics aside), pollution is easier to deal with when people are highly concentrated than when they are more spread out. The sewage must be treated in any case, and it is cheaper and more efficient to build one large treatment plant than many small ones. In addition, much less pipe and fewer pumping stations are necessary in high- than in low-density areas. In Manhattan, sewage has to be carried only a few miles to the new plant on the Hudson, while a similar project in Los Angeles, or for that matter Queens, would require great lengths of pipe. And in low density suburban areas, the costs become enormous. Thus, the cost of reducing pollution by treating sewage should be considerably less where there are high population densities.

Industrial pollution is a separate issue that is largely divorced from population. Some cities have heavy industry, others do not. A factory produces certain wastes and must treat them wherever it is located. The problem is no more serious in a city, and may actually be easier if several factories can cooperate by building common treatment plants, but industrial pollution is generally independent of population density.

This is not true of pollution due to cars. The air in and around most major urban centers is badly polluted by exhaust fumes, while less densely populated areas are relatively free of air pollution. Yet it would be misleading to conclude that the high concentration of people is responsible for this form of pollution. Indeed, quite the opposite is true. It is generally not the people who actually live in the high-density core city who do most of the driving—it is those who live in the less dense suburbs who commute to the city. In other words, the pollution is caused largely by those who do not live in the city, with the possible exception of cities like Los Angeles which are in a sense all suburb, having no substantial downtown residential area.

Indeed, if everyone lived right in the city, there would be little or no need for commuting by car. People could take rapid transit or buses, and even if they drove themselves, they would need to make only short trips that produced little exhaust fumes. In other words, although air pollution due to cars is centered around the cities, it occurs not because of but in spite of the high population density. This is not to deny that an entirely different social structure might eliminate this problem. If there were no large cities and everyone worked where he lived, there would be little commuting and also no concentrations of cars to produce too much exhaust for the air. But this is clearly not a viable alternative. The point is that air pollution is not caused by the high density in the cities, but could in fact be reduced by that factor. The major contributor is commuting by people who live around the city and work in it. In a sense, it is the suburb that has produced the problem, not the city.

Transportation. Although it is not guaranteed in the constitution, the right to cheap transportation for everyone must be an important goal of society. People who cannot move around freely are denied many of the benefits and freedoms of life. In addition, for purely economic reasons, it is essential to move people and things quickly and efficiently. One of the most serious complaints about cities is that transportation within them is tedious, slow, and expensive. Although this varies greatly from city to city, it is unquestionably true for some of them. Whereas suburbanites and those who live in smaller communities can move around town very quickly in their cars, getting around a city is often difficult.

Any city that relies on private automobiles for transportation is going to have severe congestion, as well as serious air pollution. There are simply too many people for the available roads. But the problem is neither inherent in urban living nor insoluble. Just as with air pollution, one major cause is commuting by those who do not live in the city. It is their cars that are stuck on the highways and that clog the downtown streets.

In addition, even within many cities, public transportation is so inadequate that many people must drive instead of taking the much more efficient subways, trolleys, or buses. Even so, the plight of a city dweller is actually easier than the surburbanite who commutes to the city. The latter gets up early to drive the one or two hours to work. If he is lucky and sensible, he takes a train, which is faster and easier, but still uses an hour or so. In contrast, the urbanite in a high-density city hops on the nearest bus, subway, or trolley and in most cases is at work in considerably less than an hour. It is possible to travel from practically anywhere within New York City limits to the major business areas in Manhattan in less than an hour door to door. Within the really high-density area—Manhattan—traveling time is even less. Many cities, of course, do not have such good systems, and usually those that do exist are ugly, uncomfortable, and unreliable, but sufficient funds and energy could theoretically build fast, quiet, comfortable subways which, with supplementary buses, could solve any city's transportation problem. Montreal's and Mexico City's subways are examples of what is possible. The money spent on highways during the past ten years could have built such systems for most of the major cities in the United States. It is almost a tautology that if people live closer together, transportation should be easier and cheaper. Very high density does produce the problem of congestion, but sufficient ingenuity and money should be able to solve it. In contrast, there is no clear solution to the transportation problem for suburbanites because they do, in fact, live far away and the distance must somehow be covered.

Services. Garbage collection, medical care, fire protection, power, telephone, television, newspapers, and all the other services that modern society can supply should be better and cheaper in areas of high density. The distances are smaller so that such needs as machinery, power and telephone lines, and distribution channels for newspapers and television can be concentrated. If fewer miles of lines are used, the service should be cheaper. In fact, it is well known that urbanites to some extent underwrite the costs of rural and suburban telephone and power service. In addition, hospital care can be better because it is possible to concentrate the vast resources that are now necessary for a first-rate hospital complex. A small town simply cannot afford a major hospital. The small city of New Haven can, but only because to a great extent it is also used as a training hospital for Yale University. In a low-density area, a hospital can expect to see so few cases of relatively rare conditions that it cannot afford to keep all the necessary equipment on hand, nor can it train its personnel to handle such cases. In high-density communities such as New York, there are so many hospitals that to some extent they can specialize—not all of them need to have equipment or staff to treat every condition. Furthermore, within a small radius, there are specialists for every known condition, whereas in lower-density areas they simply may not be available in the short time that may be necessary for successful treatment.

It should be clear from these brief discussions that the logistic and service problems of cities are no more serious, and may be easier to solve, than those of suburbs and small towns. Perhaps this view is overly optimistic. Even if high density should theoretically reduce the cost of solving these problems, politics may make such solution impossible. The endless squabbling among political groups in the cities certainly interferes with efficient management. The long conflict between urban, suburban, and rural populations within the United States has caused the cities to be cheated of their fair share of the tax dollar, and the enormous power of the automobile and highway lobbies has diverted money from rapid transit to an endless chain of highways.

Perhaps the most profound influence preventing the solution of the cities' problems has been an abiding pessimism. So many people believe that the cities are doomed that there has been a reluctance to expend resources or energy in what many consider a futile effort. There has been cosmetic surgery, minor attempts to keep the cities quiet or deal with some critical problem. But no long-term commitment of the vast resources that the cities need and deserve. When Mayor Lindsay of New York said some years ago that $100 billion was needed by the cities in the next ten years, most congressmen considered the figure ridiculous. Yet more than that is spent on highways. Since 70 per cent of the American people live in or around cities, the life of the city is critical for all, even the suburbanites who are often jealous of attempts to help their own central city.

Clearly, what is needed is a more optimistic and determined approach. The finding that crowding is not necessarily bad means that there is nothing inherently bad or destructive in urban life, and that therefore it might pay to try to solve the problems that do exist. The cities are worth the effort to save them. Their problems are not as bad as they are sometimes pictured, and in many cases high density is a positive rather than negative feature in solving them. The solution is not to move people out but to take advantage of the resources available within the city itself.

I say all of this as a lover of cities. I like them—but even those who do not happen to like life in the city must accept the fact that the concentration of people is not going to decline. Both groups can take hope from the findings that high concentrations do not have bad effects on people.

DENSITY AND DESIGN

Almost every major city needs new housing, not primarily for new residents—since the populations are fairly stable—but for people already living in the city who need better, more humane shelter. One controversial aspect of housing programs is the height of buildings and the population density of the area, two factors that are usually considered more or less identical. A twenty-story building will hold roughly twice as many people as a ten-story building and ten times as many as a two-story building. Assuming that the apartments are the same size and the same amount of area is covered, the taller the building, the higher the population density. Taller buildings often cover a smaller percentage of the available land because of zoning ordinances relating the height of the building to the percentage of land that can be used. If a ten-story building covers half the land it will have the same density as a five-story building that covers all of it. Thus, the height of the building and the population density of the area are not necessarily equivalent although in practice they do tend to be.

There is little doubt that many high-rise buildings designed for poor families have been failures. These public housing projects have often deteriorated rapidly, the walls and halls have been covered with graffiti, crime has been rampant, and after a while some of them have been turned into no-man's lands which even the tenants are afraid to enter. One housing development in St. Louis was such a total failure that it was eventually demolished.

This does not mean that all high-rise housing has

been unsuccessful. Many of the Mitchell-Lama cooperatives seem to be thriving; redevelopment projects in upper west side Manhattan are evidently successful, as are similar developments all over the country. Unfortunately the information necessary to evaluate this kind of housing is unavailable. Failures tend to be more widely publicized than the relative successes. It would be extremely important to have such information as how successful these high-rise developments have been and how they compare to new housing that was less tall. In the absence of such information, it is possible only to speculate on why at least some of these high-rise projects have been failures.

Two kinds of arguments have been made against high-rise public housing. The first is that they are cold, dehumanizing, and inconvenient, and discourage a sense of community. Just why all of this happens in public high-rise buildings when it does not happen in other high-rise buildings is not specified, but it is obvious that many families who live in buildings of this sort feel alienated from the rest of the people, do not make friends, do not like the modern, cold structure, and do not feel any attachment to or responsibility for the building. This lack of responsibility inevitably leads to a lack of care and eventually causes the building to become run-down. But why does this happen when the buildings are brand new, usually quite well equipped, are much more spacious—and would ordinarily be considered more pleasant—than the housing the people are used to? Why do they not like the housing, feel pride in it, and want to keep it as nice as possible? The coldness and impersonality of the building is not a sufficient answer, as these qualities are also found in buildings that do not become run-down.

The second major argument has been the high population density. When so many people are crowded into a small area, so the argument goes, they suffer all kinds of ill effects. They become anxious and afraid, they are aggressive and violent, they suffer physical and mental breakdowns, they become defensive and withdrawn, and so on. When so many people live in one building, they cannot feel a common bond, cannot feel that the building is theirs personally. Thus, there is the worst possible combination: a feeling of anonymity and impersonality together with fear and aggressiveness.

Although this may in fact happen under some circumstances, it is not the typical response to high population density. There is no evidence that such responses or any other negative responses are a standard, normal reaction to crowding. Rather, according to the density-intensity theory here proposed, crowding intensifies the typical reactions, whatever they might be. How can this theory explain the occasional failure of high-rise public housing, and how can it be of use in preventing such failures in the future?

When the social situation is bad, when people feel cut off, defensive, afraid, and suspicious, high population density will aggravate the already bad situation. Living in a high-rise building with hundreds of other families will intensify all of these negative feelings. Poor people often feel isolated, that they are powerless, that they are subject to forces totally beyond their control. Living in a twenty-story building with hundreds of other families should exaggerate these feelings—particularly in a cold, modern structure with, as is usually the case, relatively poor maintenance and services. If there is any vandalism or crime in the building, people who already feel isolated and weak will feel doubly anxious and afraid. The high density will increase their fear, which in turn will magnify their suspicion of their neighbors, which will reinforce their feeling of isolation. The spiral of isolation, friendlessness, crime, and more isolation continues until the building becomes uninhabitable.

On the other hand, if the situation can be structured so that people do not feel this sense of isolation, if they feel friendly and open in the first place, if they get to know and trust their neighbors, the high density should intensify these positive feelings. A high-rise building which has good espirit de corps, in which people know each other and work together, can provide a healthy, vital environment in which to live. Conditions of high density can have positive effects and need not have negative ones. The problem is to design buildings (whether high-rise or not) that foster positive reactions which will then be intensified by the high density.

It seems to me—and at this point I am admittedly getting more and more speculative—that the crucial element in designing a building should be to foster and encourage close social interaction among the residents. The great advantage of a four-story walk-up is that almost everyone eventually meets everyone else. They may not all like each other, and some may even be afraid of some of the others, but they are not living among strangers.

This has powerful effects because no one feels or is anonymous. If anyone writes on the walls, leaves garbage in the hall, lets his apartment run down, or in any other way fails to live up to his responsibilities, everyone knows. There is ample evidence that people who feel anonymous are more antisocial and less under normal social controls. Breaking down the anonymity will cause everyone to act more responsibly. In addition, it makes it much harder for people who do not live in the building to commit acts of vandalism or crime. Just as the residents are no longer anonymous, any stranger immediately stands out. People can still sneak into the building and commit crimes, of course, but they are much more likely to be noticed, to be recognized as strangers, and to be watched. Finally, when there is a sense of community, people are more likely to give assistance should a mugging or some other act of violence occur.

Once it is recognized that encouraging social interaction and close interpersonal relations is one of the most crucial aspects of housing, it becomes possible to design new housing with that in mind. It is clear that much of the high-rise housing built in the last ten or twenty years is poorly designed from this point of view. A twenty-story building with long corridors shared by twenty families and with no public spaces except on the street floor does not encourage social interaction. Two huge elevators for four hundred families may be efficient, but the people riding those elevators are not as likely to get to know each other as they are in an elevator shared by twenty families.

Similarly, a long corridor with many families on it

discourages close interactions. The longer the corridor, the less familiar each family will be with the others on it, the less likely they will be to become friendly, and most important, the smaller the chance that the floor as a whole will develop a feeling of closeness and community.

This leads to a more general point, which is that having to interact or deal with large *numbers* of people generally seems to have negative effects. To begin with, it is somewhat overwhelming. Too much is unpredictable, there are too many faces, too many possible contacts for most people to handle. The whole situation more or less gets out of hand and we feel that it is beyond our control. Whether in a playground with hundreds of children or an apartment house corridor with thirty apartments, the typical reaction is to withdraw and be defensive. There is an important difference between large numbers of people and a high density of people. A large playground with two hundred children may have a lower population density than a small playground with fifty, but it is the former that is overwhelming, not the latter.

In addition, large numbers of people discourage close social interaction and a feeling of community, not only because the individual feels overwhelmed and isolated—but also simply because of the mechanics of the situation. If you see thirty people regularly, it is much easier to get to know them than if you see two hundred people regularly. When you share an elevator with four people, they become individuals whom you can interact with; when there are twenty-five people in the elevator, you cannot even see all their faces much less get to know them as people.

Therefore, many of the difficulties in high-rise housing would be helped by breaking up the corridors into separate units and providing elevators for each of them. Immediately, the chance of making friends in the elevators is increased because fewer people are sharing them. More important, when there are only six or seven families on a corridor, it is almost impossible for them not to get to know each other, and friendships are more likely to spring up. Obviously this is expensive, but it is far better than having to destroy the building because it has deteriorated. In any case, the reason for putting up these buildings is presumably to provide good housing for those who need it; if it costs a little more, it is still worth it. I would not, by the way, make these corridors too small. When there are only two or three families on a floor, once again the sense of isolation and lack of community might be encouraged. Although people will be very likely to get to know their neighbors, there are so few neighbors that it is hard to develop a sense of community. It is impossible to say what the ideal number is, but a rough guess is that it is considerably smaller than twenty and somewhat larger than four. I am not by any means claiming that breaking up the corridors will solve all the problems, but it will encourage a sense of community and pride and will break down the anonymity that is so dangerous and destructive.

Other parts of the building can also be designed to encourage rather than discourage the tenants to interact with each other. There seems to be almost a deliberate attempt to make each person's apartment a fortress; many inhabitants of high-rise, low-cost housing are like caged animals, making forays from their nests to get food or clothing and then returning to "safety." Isolationism has never worked very well for countries, and it certainly does not work for individuals. The way to have a safe, comfortable, full life is to interact with neighbors, to know other people around you, and to be part of a community (making full allowance for those who prefer total privacy). Whether or not this is a deliberate goal of the architects, the design of most new buildings does have the effect of discouraging interactions. People are given no convenient place to interact. Although almost every building provides some kind of playground or public area, it is generally located on the ground floor regardless of the height of the building. A twenty-story building might have one public area where presumably children can play while parents talk to each other and watch. Not only is it a bad idea to have only one very large area, but locating it on the ground floor is inconvenient for most of the people in the building.

Once again it is the size of the area and the corresponding number of people involved which discourages interaction. Thus, at the very least, there should be a number of smaller play areas perhaps designed for a given section of the building so that the same people will use them each day. If for some reason this is not feasible, having smaller units will encourage more interaction. Naturally it is desirable to have at least one fairly large area for games that require plenty of space, such as basketball, but most of the activities that children and adults engage in can be pursued in quite small areas.

Having all of these areas on the ground floor, while understandable, is unfortunate. This arrangement is suitable when the child has plenty of time, but the psychological and practical difficulties of riding down fifteen stories for a few minutes of activity discourages informal, spontaneous play.

The problem is even more serious for the parents. They have responsibilities in the home, cooking or cleaning or other work. Whatever they do, it is often difficult to leave the apartment for a long period of time. In small buildings, they can look out the window and watch their children playing and thus provide some kind of supervision. In a tall building where the play areas are all on the ground, the parents can supervise only by leaving the apartment. Thus, children are either not allowed to play or end up playing largely without any supervision.

Another solution to the problem of encouraging social interaction, providing a sense of community, and at the same time allowing convenient supervision of children would be to have social areas for each floor or set of floors. For example, if a floor has a long corridor broken up into three subunits, an area of a few hundred square feet might be set aside in the central unit. Or if the three subunits on each corridor are not interconnected, such areas might be provided for the smaller units, with one on every three floors. Such an area is obviously expensive—it takes space that could be used for two bedrooms or a good-sized living room—but it might have positive social effects.

This area could have three separate functions. In the

first place, it should contain useful appliances such as washers and driers. Every building must provide an area for these, but in low-cost housing (and even some higher-cost housing) they are usually located in the basement, which is not only inconvenient but tends to become a neglected and therefore an unpleasant area, certainly not considered part of any individual's or group of individuals' domain.

In contrast, a small area on the same or an adjacent floor is not only convenient but becomes a place to meet one's neighbors. I once lived in a building that provided such an area on each floor. Although no one ever spent any time in the room since it was barely large enough to stand in, it did become a place for meeting one's neighbors, and doing one's wash became a less frustrating and time-consuming operation because people would help each other out by transferring a wash to the drier or knocking on a neighbor's door to tell him the machine was ready, and so on. In such a situation, even waiting becomes pleasant or at least bearable as it provides an opportunity for informal social interaction—the type of interaction that public-housing designers should be striving for.

The space should be large enough so that at least young children can play in it. The area should be provided with some simple toys, perhaps a cushioned floor so that the children won't hurt themselves, and whatever else may make it a pleasant place for the children to play in. Finally, it would be highly desirable if there were some minimal refreshments, such as coffee and Coke machines, and perhaps even something more elaborate. If thirty families shared the facilities, all of this should be feasible, although the refreshment machines would probably have to be subsidized or owned and operated by the building itself.

This combination of play area, utility area, and refreshment stand might provide a base for informal social interaction. People would meet informally while doing their wash, while supervising their children, or while simply having a Coke or a cup of coffee. Cooperation would be almost automatic, leading to much greater familiarity among the tenants, the development of friendships, and almost certainly a sense of community. People would regard this little area as theirs, to use and to take care of. Because it was there, it would produce more traffic in the halls, and the sense of community would probably extend to the halls themselves. It would encourage a sense of ownership of at least a part of the building, would cause the unit sharing it to be more cohesive, and combined with a breaking up of the long corridors, would lead to a greater sense of community interaction.

This view is admittedly somewhat idealized. Some buildings have provided social areas on each floor and they have not always been successful. In some buildings they have become gathering places for undesirable people or centers for crime, and on occasion have apparently become so dangerous that they had to be chained shut. But the failure of some of these public spaces does not imply that they are a bad idea. If the morale and general atmosphere of the building are bad, it is unlikely that any minor change such as providing a social space on the floor will help much. On the other hand, if the rest of the structure is such as to encourage good morale and social interaction, such a place could have very beneficial effects.

All of this is expensive. Although the amount of space necessary for such a social area is not enormous, it is considerable: however, this space could be obtained by decreasing the size of the apartments without producing any negative effects. In fact, the whole question of how large rooms should be is very much open. There is not the slightest evidence that larger rooms are healthier or lead to greater satisfaction. In his massive study of Hong Kong, R. E. Mitchell found that the amount of space per person in an apartment was unrelated to any measure of stress or nervousness, and all of the research on crowding suggests the same. Many wealthy people prefer what they call a small, intimate apartment to a more spacious one. This is perhaps a matter of esthetic preference, but there is no evidence that small rooms have negative effects on their occupants. If making the rooms somewhat smaller would allow the building to have public play areas such as those described above, it would be more than worth the exchange. No one suffers from having somewhat smaller rooms, but people do suffer from a lack of social interaction and feeling of community. Given a choice, space should be taken from the apartments and put into carefully designed, semipublic space. This mixing of public and private space is absolutely crucial in the encouraging of social interaction in the building.

All these suggestions have been concerned with minimizing the negative effects of high-rise housing. The setting that these suggestions are intended to produce is already present in smaller housing, such as a four-story building with short corridors. In the smaller building people are grouped in manageable units, they get to know one another on stairs or in the smaller elevators, they have easy access to ground floor play and social areas, and in general informal social interaction is easy and natural. It is almost impossible for people to live in such a building without getting to know one another. In addition, because it is a smaller unit, there is a tendency to feel more responsible for all of it and to have a sense of ownership that is often lacking in a larger structure. When only twenty families live in a building, it belongs to all of them; when two hundred do, it belongs to none of them. Thus, it is much easier to make low-rise housing good because it does not have many of the negative aspects inherent in high-rise housing.

This does not mean that all high-rise housing should be eliminated. Sometimes the economic considerations demand the maximum use of the available space, and only a tall building will qualify. If the building is designed well, it can be a healthy place to live. But whenever possible, lower housing should be favored because it is more likely to be successful.

It is extremely important to realize that there is no reason to avoid high density in this low-rise housing. As W. H. Whyte has described in detail, the total density is often no higher for tall buildings than for low ones. If a four-story building covers the entire piece of land, it can have as high density as an eight-story building that covers only half. The former is preferable, as open land is not crucial, particularly since people should be encouraged to use the streets rather than inner courtyards anyway. The point is that arguments against high-rise housing in terms of population density are wrong, but arguments based on social considerations are right. High density, whether in low- or high-rise buildings, is fine as long as the design is good. However, since designs are not always good and changes in structures cannot always overcome inherent difficulties, low-rise housing is more likely to be successful.

Let me be clear that I am proposing two quite different goals for new housing. First, it should provide clean, efficient, well-organized, pleasant apartments for the residents, with enough rooms so that a moderate amount of privacy is possible. But I think the amount of space is relatively unimportant; the number of rooms and their design are more important than their size. It may even be that a small living room is preferable to a large one; a combined living, dining, and even kitchen area to a larger, more separate one. And my own guess is that whenever there is a choice between, say, three large bedrooms and four small ones, the latter is preferable. There should be enough space to provide all of the equipment and privacy that is necessary, but beyond that it is not even clear that space is a positive feature. Secondly, the buildings should provide an environment that encourages social interaction and a sense of community. This must be done by breaking up the unit into manageable size, by providing social areas in which people meet informally, and by doing everything possible to make the people feel that it is their building, that some of the space outside their apartment belongs to them and to their neighbors, and to make them feel responsible for and proprietary toward it. Otherwise people live in comfortable but isolated cells rather than in a community.

The sense of isolation that is felt even by many wealthy people in New York City is probably produced by this lack of interaction within high-rise buildings. In designing new space, it is essential that a major emphasis be placed on breaking down isolation. Whenever these two goals of providing an adequate apartment and encouraging social interaction conflict, priority should be given to the latter rather than the former. Extra frills, extra rooms, extra space within the apartment probably have little effect on the residents; but extra elevators, extra social areas, anything that encourages the use of public space has enormous effects.

The same is true for groups of buildings: In order to encourage people who live in an area to think of it as a neighborhood and have a sense of community, everything possible should be done to facilitate social interaction within the community. Neighborhood parks and refreshment areas play a role, provided they are not allowed to become areas of conflict and destruction rather than centers of positive activity.

There is no easy method for achieving this goal, but density of use is one crucial variable. A large, open park that is sparsely used does not have the protection of many eyes and bodies, and the people who use it are generally anonymous and strangers to one another. Under these circumstances, a sense of community rarely develops. The park becomes run-down, people do not take care of it, and strangers can easily enter it to commit vandalism and crimes.

One of John V. Lindsay's most notable accomplishments as mayor of New York was to open Central Park to the public once again. He did this by encouraging bike riding, providing all sorts of entertainment activities both day and night, and generally attracting large numbers of people to the park. As a result, it is no longer a dangerous place to be, it is no longer a haven for criminals and deviants. The crime rate during the day in heavily used areas is quite low, and the presence of policemen is less crucial than it used to be. The park is now a healthy environment widely used and enjoyed.

The same can be accomplished in a small park or play area if people are encouraged to use it. There should be refreshment stands, play areas, water fountains, and activities of all kinds. If people are drawn to the area, they in turn draw others and the park becomes a lively, active place.

The area should not be too large relative to the number of people for whom it is convenient. Central Park serves virtually all of Manhattan and even so, parts of it are usually deserted. Those parts are dangerous, while the more highly used ones are not. Many people would probably prefer a low-density use of the park, but the purpose of urban parks is not to provide places to be alone to enjoy the beauties of nature. Urban parks and recreational areas are for informal, relaxed use, and the most successful are those with quite a high level of density.

Once this is accepted, it can be readily seen that neighborhood social areas should be designed to encourage high-density use. A social area containing one or two basketball courts, a play area for young children, lots of benches, and a refreshment stand is almost certainly better than one containing two or three times as much space because it would provide higher-density usage and therefore a safer, livelier arena. Just as cutting the size of a corridor in a building encourages closer social interaction, so does decreasing the size of a playground. The same is true of community centers, schools, churches, and other places where people tend to meet. Everything possible should be done to break up populations into relatively small groups of people without producing divisions or splinter groups, so as to encourage close interaction within the groups.

Many of the positive features of urban life depend on both large population and high density. Neither alone can provide diversity, stimulation, and opportunity. Life in New York City would not be duplicated by 7 million people scattered evenly over Montana or seven thousand living under very high density in a tiny town. On the other hand, the two aspects of urban life have quite different consequences. Whereas high density does not have generally negative effects on people and can even intensify positive aspects of a social situation, it does seem that a large number of people has some inherently negative effects. The anonymity, sense of isolation, and difficulty of dealing with many people at once are usually harmful. The anonymity can also be beneficial in allowing the individual greater freedom of action and expression, but by and large, the psychological effects of vast numbers of people are probably more bad than good.

Therefore, one approach to urban problems is to minimize the effects of numbers while maximizing the positive effects of high density. This can be done by setting up as many situations as possible in which relatively small groups of people interact under conditions of high density, and by reducing the anonymity of the city by bringing the same people together as often as possible under these high-density conditions. It has been pointed out how this can be done in housing developments, playgrounds, parks, and other public facilities. These measures will also tend to reduce crime. Pockets will probably still be picked and no one will interfere with the numbers racket because almost no one considers it a crime, but the crimes most people worry about, such as mugging, robbery, rape, and assault, are much less likely to occur when there are other people around.

The same holds true for city streets. The more they are used, the safer they will be. Unfortunately some buildings and communities are designed to keep people off the streets, on the theory that, since people get mugged on the streets, they should be kept safely in their apartments or enclosed courtyards. This is absolutely the wrong approach to the problem. The reason streets are dangerous is not because there are too many people on them, but because there are too few.

Housing and communities should be designed so as to encourage the use of streets and sidewalks as much as possible. Inner courtyards should be eliminated or minimized. People tend not to use them because they are so uninteresting, and when they do use them they will not be on the streets outside where the action really is. A healthy building is one with plenty of activity in front of it, where people watch each other and get to know each other, and a sense of community can develop. There is no reason why this cannot happen in an inner courtyard, but when it does, the courtyard becomes an island in the city rather than relating directly to the rest of the community. The people who live in the building must rush through the dangerous streets in order, finally, to find refuge within the walls of their building (prison). In contrast, if all of the doors open onto the street and the streets can be made lively and safe, people need not rush through streets to find safe havens. The streets themselves become safe, and the community obviously is much more vital and alive.

It is important that people have reasons for being out on the streets. There should be all sorts of shopping and activities within easy range of housing. When there is an all-night newspaper stand, people will leave their apartments to get newspapers. When there is a convenient neighborhood grocery store, people will walk to shop. This not only provides the convenience of easy shopping, but perhaps more important encourages the kind of traffic which makes the streets both interesting and safe.

A combination of playgrounds, parks, and other recreational areas which have high-density use, relatively private playgrounds attached to specific buildings but which border on the street, and neighborhood stores and newsstands will bring the people out of their apartments and onto the streets. In this way people will get to know each other better, there will be a sense of an active lively community, and the streets will be safer.

When the streets have few people on them, crime rate goes up and more people stay off the streets because they are afraid, which causes even more crime. As fewer people go out, stores and newsstands close earlier, which causes still fewer people to go out, which makes the newsstands close even earlier.

It is not true that there is nothing to fear but fear itself, but it is true that once people are afraid of being on the street, this fear in fact makes the street dangerous. There is a self-fulfilling prophecy—you are afraid of the streets so you stay off them, so they become dangerous, thus providing a reason to be afraid of them. One goal should be to break this cycle of fear and crime by bringing people onto the streets and making them less dangerous. This will reverse the spiral, encouraging more people to come into the streets and further reducing the crime rate.

11 CONCLUSIONS

The changes proposed in the foregoing chapters are not by themselves going to solve the severe problems of housing and crime and general dissatisfaction with urban life. Obviously, social and economic problems such as poverty, prejudice, and immorality in government must be eliminated before the crimes they generate disappear. The structural changes suggested, however, can have substantial positive effects. Poor people living in public housing are always going to be dissatisfied, but encouraging social interaction and a sense of community can reduce that dissatisfaction and make the housing a more vital healthy place to live. The same is true of city streets. There will always be crime until the other problems are solved, but the streets can be active and interesting rather than deserted and dangerous.

More generally, it is absolutely crucial to recognize that high density is going to exist for the foreseeable future. Fighting the population explosion by encouraging a decrease in birthrate, discovering better and easier methods of birth control, and making people aware of the problem is extremely important. But it is unrealistic and fortunately unnecessary to worry about the possibility of depopulating the major urban centers. People have always concentrated in the cities and unless society undergoes an almost unimaginable change, there will continue to be high concentrations of people.

Many planners, urban specialists, and city dwellers fail to recognize that life in the city is different from life in the suburbs or country. They want the city to have features of the country that it simply cannot have. People complain that it is difficult to get a sense of peace and relaxation in the city, that the parks are either dangerous or too crowded, that houses almost never have lovely, peaceful, private gardens in which people can be alone and enjoy the outdoors. They complain that the most attractive, interesting areas of the city immediately become popular and are then no longer peaceful.

These complaints are foolish; cities cannot have certain features of the country as it is the essence of a city to have large populations concentrated in fairly small areas. Any failure to recognize and accept this condition is ridiculous. Only by accepting both the positive and negative sides of city life, emphasizing the former and trying to minimize the latter, can the cities be utilized and enjoyed. There is no point complaining that there are too many people around—that is what makes a city a city. Good transportation and other facilities must be provided so that the presence of all these people is not oppressive, so that they interfere with each other as little as possible. But it is unrealistic to try to produce situations where the people aren't present. Rather than attempting to provide spacious gardens or solitude in search of some impossible pastoral existence, building design should encourage healthy, lively contact among neighbors.

It is perhaps even more important that people recognize that high density does not have negative effects on humans. At times it seems as if urban planners, social philosophers, and strong forces in the American government have thrown up their hands in despair and written off the cities as hopeless. They feel that they have to spend a certain amount of money on urban problems, but basically regard this as money down the drain. This attitude is understandable, given a belief in the destructive effects of high density. But, as I have demonstrated throughout the book, the cities' problems are not due to high density; if the cities can be made healthy, pleasant places to live in, the high density will enhance the positive aspects of city living and the cities can continue to be what they have been in the past—dynamic, vital forces.

APPENDIXES

Much of the research reported in chapters 5, 7, and 8 was conducted by the author with various collaborators. Although the general methods and major results of these studies are described in the text, these appendixes present additional aspects of procedure and results, including technical details of statistical analyses and tables. Some of this work has already been published and the references are given for those who wish to see more extensive reports.

Appendix 1: Population Density and Pathology in Metropolitan Areas (In Collaboration with Stanley Heshka and Alan Levy)

Method: Data are taken from the ninety-seven standard metropolitan statistical areas (SMSA) for which all figures were available, excluding New York City and Jersey City because their densities were so much greater than any other comparable areas. (Removing these two points did not appreciably affect the results.)

Independent variables are population per square mile, median annual income, percent with income below $3000 a year, percent nonwhite, median years of school completed, total population, and total per capita expenditure by local governments. Dependent variables are overall crime rate and individual rates for murder, rape, robbery, assault, burglary, and car theft. Data are taken from the *Statistical Abstract of the United States* for 1970.

Results: The first step was to correlate the crime rate with density, population, income, and percent nonwhite. Table 1 shows that there is a substantial and significant relationship between density and overall crime, robbery, and car theft. In all cases, some other variable is more strongly related to the crime measure, but at this level higher density does go along with higher crimes in these categories.

Table 1: Correlations of Crime with Density, Population, Income, and Per Cent Nonwhite in SMSAs

	DENSITY	POPULATION	INCOME	% NONWHITE
Over-all Crime (15)	.300*	.376*	.194	.313*
Murder (16)	.072	.180	−.361*	.627*
Rape (17)	.124	.336*	.078	.226*
Assault (19)	.056	.201*	−.235*	.425*
Robbery (18)	.457*	.578*	.312*	.242*
Burglary (20)	.182	.247*	.035	.323*
Car Theft (21)	.446*	.480*	.362*	.250*

* $p < .05$

The next step was to compute a stepwise multiple regression which indicates what factor is most strongly related to crime rate and also the order of importance of all factors. When this was done, density was not among the first five variables for any of the categories of crime and never explained an appreciable amount of variance. In other words, when other factors are controlled, density is no longer related to crime rate.

Appendix 2: Population Density and Pathology in New York City (In Collaboration with Stanley Heshka and Alan Levy)

Method: The data are drawn primarily from the 1965 *New York City Directory of Needs* which relies heavily on the 1960 census. This directory includes demographic and health statistics for each of the 338 Health Areas of the city (we used only 334 since data were incomplete for 4). Each health area is a reasonably homogeneous neighborhood of 15,000–25,000 residents.

Independent variables: There are four measures of income—median income, per cent of households earning below $3000 a year, per cent between $3000 and $3999, and per cent above $10,000. These measures are closely related and we have generally relied on median income as the single best indicator of the economic level of the area. There are three measures of ethnic composition—per cent of the population that is Puerto Rican, per cent nonwhite (not including Puerto Rican), and per cent white. We have generally relied on the last measure as a convenient index of ethnic mix of the area. Age distribution is described by three measures—per cent under 18, per cent between 18 and 64, and per cent 65 and over. Also, there are measures of median education level achieved, unemployment rate, number of substandard housing units as a percentage of total units, per cent of population that changed residence in the last two years, ratio of males to females, and rate of unrelated individuals living together.

Population density is indicated by two measures. The number of persons per residential acre describes the overall density within the area. This measure excludes land used for parks, highways, and industrial use. Household crowding is measured by the average number of persons per room in all household units in the area.

Dependent variables: Crime rate is indicated by the number of juvenile offenses recorded per 100,000 juveniles for 1965 and 1966 and the number of arrests per juvenile for 1965. These three measures are closely related and we relied mainly on the first, using the others primarily as a check on the stability of the indicators. Juvenile delinquency was used rather than adult crime not only because better statistics are available but also because it is a more sensitive indicator of aggressiveness since adult crime is more likely to involve purely economic motives. Note that the figures are for the offense committed by juveniles *living* in the area, whether or not the offenses are committed in the area. There are two measures of mental health—number of admissions to state mental institutions and number of terminations of psychiatric treatment recorded by city agencies. In addition, we included the number of children born out of wedlock per 1000 women of child-bearing age, the rate of infant mortality, and the rate of incidence of venereal disease.

Results: The major independent variables are substantially related. Table 2.1 presents the intercorrelations of the two measures of density and income and ethnicity. The two measures of density are only moderately related—density per acre does not necessarily coincide with density per room. This is particularly true of New York City, where many affluent people live in high-rise buildings in areas of very high density but with very large apartments, and where some relatively poor people live in lower buildings having very crowded rooms. However, in general, poorer people and nonwhites do live in high-density areas and in crowded apartments, as shown by the strong negative correlations between both measures of density and indicators of income and per cent whites.

Table 2.1: Intercorrelations among Independent Variables

	DENSITY 1	DENSITY 2	INCOME	ETHNICITY
Density (acre)	—	.383	−.515	−.485
Density (room)		—	−.659	−.523
Income (median)			—	.719
Ethnicity (% whites)				—

The next step was to compute correlations between these four major independent variables and the six major measures of pathology. As can be seen in Table 2.2, density, income, and ethnicity are all substantially related to all forms of pathology. The higher the density, the greater the incidence of pathology, with the pattern being approximately the same for both measures of density. It should be noted, however, that correlations with income and ethnicity are in almost all cases higher than with density. Since income and ethnicity are likely to be important causal factors leading to juvenile delinquency and the other pathologies, it is important to separate the effects of these basic social factors from that of density.

Table 2.2: Correlations between Dependent and Independent Variables

	JUVENILE DELINQUENCY	HOSPITAL ADMISSIONS	PSYCHIATRIC TERMINATIONS	VENEREAL DISEASE	INFANT MORTALITY	UNMARRIED BIRTHS
Density 1	.356	.402	.555	.549	.282	.559
Density 2	.429	.318	.532	.318	.410	.471
Income	−.668	−.499	−.602	−.498	−.494	−.692
Ethnicity	−.752	−.549	−.691	−.689	−.563	−.881

This was attempted by computing two multiple regression analyses in which the unconfounded influence of each factor could be assessed. In the first analysis, all variables were allowed to enter where they would, no assumptions being made as to priority. In the second analysis, income and ethnicity were entered first in order to assess the effect of density separate from these critical factors. Table 2.3 presents the results of the first multiple regression. It can be seen that the two measures of density explain little of the variance in our measures of pathology. When other factors are controlled in this

Table 2.3: Amount of Variance Explained with Step Density Entered in Stepwise Multiple Regression

	JUVENILE DELINQUENCY	HOSPITAL ADMISSIONS	PSYCHIATRIC TERMINATIONS	VENEREAL DISEASE	INFANT MORTALITY	UNMARRIED BIRTHS
Density 1						
Variance (%)	0.2	0.7	6.3	0.1	0.1	0.3
Step entered	10	6	2	—	—	9
Density 2						
Variance (%)	0.4	0.1	1.3	0.2	0.5	0.1
Step entered	8	—	4	6	5	—

way, neither density per acre nor household crowding account for an appreciable amount of variation in any of the measures, with the possible exception of psychiatric terminations where density per acre explains a modest 6.3 per cent. The second multiple regression is shown in Table 2.4 for delinquency and psychiatric terminations. Although ethnicity and income explain large amounts of variance, density adds little or nothing, although once again it is slightly related to psychiatric terminations.

Table 2.4: Amount of Variance Explained in Stepwise Multiple Regression with Income and Ethnicity Entered First

	JUVENILE DELINQUENCY	PSYCHIATRIC TERMINATIONS
Density 1	0.4	4.8
Density 2	0.3	2.1
Income	44.7	36.2
Ethnicity	15.2	13.8

These multiple regressions are attempts to control statistically for income and ethnicity and other factors in order to assess the effect of density per se. This kind of statistical control must be interpreted cautiously. There is always the chance that density is the critical variable, and income and ethnicity less important. Even though they explain more variance than density, it might be that density is a causal factor. To assess this possibility more directly, we took advantage of the fact that we had many more data points than are usually available in this kind of study. Because there are 334 health areas, we could examine only those areas that have equal incomes. If density does affect juvenile delinquency, those areas with higher density should have higher juvenile delinquency. That is, among only poor neighborhoods or moderate-income neighborhoods or rich neighborhoods, the greater the density, the higher should be the juvenile delinquency. No fancy statistical controls are necessary—we can look at a large number of equal-income areas and assess the effect of density.

Table 2.5: Correlations between Density, Juvenile Delinquency, and Psychiatric Terminations within Income Levels

	MEDIAN INCOME			
	$3000–4999 N = 86	*$5000–5999* N = 64	*$6000–6999* N = 105	*$7000 and Up* N = 74
Density 1 and JD	−.268	−.141	−.137	.045
Density 2 and JD	−.081	.146	−.159	.004
Density 1 and PT	.300	.330	.182	.342
Density 2 and PT	.132	.245	.258	.362

This analysis is shown in Table 2.5. It can be seen that density is either unrelated or actually negatively related to juvenile delinquency. All of the correlations are small, with the biggest being negative. Within poor neighborhoods higher density is associated with somewhat lower rates of juvenile delinquency; within moderate and high-income areas there is essentially no relationship at all. This seems to be convincing evidence that density is not a factor producing juvenile delinquency. A similar analysis for psychiatric terminations indicates that density continues to have slight correlations with this measure. Thus, although there is substantial reason to believe that density is unrelated to juvenile delinquency, venereal disease, infant mortality, unmarried births, and admission to mental hospitals, it may have some association with relatively minor mental disturbances even when income is controlled.

Appendix 3: The Effect of Crowding on Task Performance (In Collaboration with Simon Klevansky and Paul Ehrlich)*

Method A: The subjects were 126 high school students, 84 males and 42 females, recruited through an ad in the *Palo Alto Times* offering $1.75 an hour for a ten-hour experiment. Groups consisted of either all males or all females and had either five or nine members. There were three rooms containing 160, 80, and 35 square feet. We assumed that both the five-member and nine-member groups would be crowded in the smallest room and neither would be in the largest room. The middle room was used as an additional condition to assess the relationship between size and number. The rooms were comfortably air-conditioned and had sound-proofed walls to reduce noise levels. Subjects sat on comfortable chairs that had writing arms.

All subjects came for a one-hour instruction session on a Monday and then participated for three hours on each of the next three days. Groups were randomly assigned to one of the three rooms the first full day of the experiment, and then moved to the other rooms during the next two days. Thus, each group worked in each size room.

Each experimental session consisted of the following tasks: (1) The group discussed a current problem for twenty minutes to get the members acquainted and accustomed to the room. (2) Subjects crossed out all of a particular number that appeared on a sheet of numbers for ten minutes. (3) They formed words from six letters that were read to them. Two different sets were read and they worked on each for eight minutes. (4) They tried to think of as many uses for a common object as they could (e.g., a 10-gallon barrel). This is often used as a test of creative thinking. It took ten minutes. (5) Twelve common words were read at the rate of one per second and each subject was asked to write down as many as he could remember when the list was completed. Eight such lists were read, with a thirty-second pause between lists. (6) The subjects were given a concentration task in which clicks were sounded at the rate of about three per second in varying rhythms and the subject had merely to count them. The number of clicks ranged from fifteen to fifty-seven, and it is harder than it may sound. (7) The object-uses task was given again, this time with the group as a whole working on it.

This sequence was followed by a ten-minute break and then the complete series was repeated with different materials.

* These experiments are described fully in Freedman, Klevansky & Ehrlich, 1971.

Over the three days different materials were used, but the same sequence was kept.

Results: No effects of room size or number in the group were found. On no task was any room appreciably better than any other; neither at the beginning of the series nor toward the end, on the first day or the last, taking just the first day or just any other day, no matter how the data are analyzed was there any effect of density or number.

Method B: Subjects were 306 high school students divided into 34 groups ranging in size from seven to nine. Eighteen of the groups were all male, sixteen all female. Each group took part in two sessions—one in the large room and one in the small room. The moderate-sized room was not used.

The procedure was similar to the first study except that subjects worked on only three tasks—crossing out numbers for two hours, forming words for ten minutes, and solving anagrams (forming words out of scrambled letters) for fifty minutes. We also manipulated motivation by telling half of the groups that if they did well, they would be paid an additional $7.50.

Results: There were no effects of room size on performance. The high motivation subjects did somewhat better on the crossing-out task and somewhat less well on the more creative forming words and anagram tasks, but none of these effects are significant.

Method C: The previous study was repeated using a different population of subjects. Instead of high school students, the participants were 180 women between the ages of twenty-five and sixty who were recruited through a temporary employment agency. They worked for four hours a day for two days, in either the small or large room.

Results: As in the other studies, there were absolutely no effects of room size on task performance.

Appendix 4: Crowding and Competitiveness (In Collaboration with Michael Katz and Donald Kinder) *

Method: Groups of four subjects of the same sex were put in either large (72.25 square feet) or small (25 square feet) rooms. The subjects were 136 high school students from Palo Alto, California: 72 females and 64 males, who were recruited through a newspaper advertisement and paid $8.00 for the four-hour experiment. Participants sat in comfortable chairs that had writing arms. In the small room each chair was placed with its back against the middle of one of the walls.

* This experiment is described fully in Freedman et al., 1972.

This allowed just enough room so that the knees of one subject did not quite touch those of another. In the larger room, the format was the same except that the chairs were placed a few feet in from the walls.

Subjects were first given forty minutes to become acquainted with one another. Next they spent about an hour discussing two topics of interest to them; how much freedom students should have in terms of choosing courses, and how to prevent students from dropping out of school. During the third hour they played the labryrinth game in pairs. This is a maze game in which the goal is to maneuver a small ball along a path between holes. The ball is controlled by tilting the board by means of two knobs. Ordinarily one person handles both knobs, but we had two subjects each manipulate one. This makes the coordination even more difficult. Within each room, one pair competed with the other pair in order to score higher (i.e., move the ball farther along the maze without allowing it to fall into a hole). The game was played for twenty trials and the team was given ten cents for each trial on which they scored higher. This game was included primarily to force the subjects to interact closely.

The major part of the study consisted of another game in which subjects could either compete or cooperate with one another. This was a variation of the prisoner's dilemma situation in which all four subjects made choices instead of only two people. The rules were as follows: If all subjects selected blue, they would each win 20¢; if three chose blue and one red, the three would each lose 50¢ and the other would win $1.50; if they split two and two, those choosing blue received 20¢ and those choosing red lost 10¢; if they split one blue, three red, the blue gained 50¢ and the reds each lost 30¢; and if they all chose red, they each lost 20¢. It is somewhat difficult to compare this game to standard two-man variations. In the latter, on any one trial it is typically more desirable to choose red than blue regardless of your partner's choice, but over a series of trials the most successful strategy is for both members to choose blue consistently. That, of course, is what produces the dilemma. In the four-man game there is no obviously dominant choice on any trial. It is tempting to choose red in the hopes of everyone else picking blue, but it is better in the long run for everyone to pick blue on every trial. Whatever the optimal strategy, it is clear that picking blue is a more cooperative and less competitive choice than picking red. Therefore, blue choices are considered indications of cooperation and red choices of competition.

All choices were private and anonymous, signaled by

pressing a button on a box on the subject's table, but after each trial the experimenter announced how much each subject had won or lost, so that it was fairly obvious what everyone had selected once the trial was over. Subjects were allowed to talk before each trial, but not to announce their choices. The game was run for twenty trials and subjects were not told ahead of time how long it would last.

Results: There were no effects of room size on the discussion sessions or the labyrinth game. The number and quality of ideas in the discussions did not differ systematically, nor did the total scores, amounts of money won, maximum score achieved, variance in scores, or the difference between the two teams on the maze game. The only reliable difference on these two tasks is that male subjects did significantly better than females on the labyrinth game.

The major focus of the study was on the amount of competition in the prisoner's dilemma game. These results are presented in Table 4.1, which shows the mean number of competitive choices as a function of room size and sex of subject. An analysis of variance is shown in Table 4.2. Two results are

Table 4.1: Number of Competitive Choices as a Function of Room Size and Sex

ROOM SIZE	MALES	FEMALES
Large	29.87*	44.56
Small	44.62	36.56

* Maximum score is 80.

Table 4.2: Analysis of Variance for Table 4.1

SOURCE	DF	MS	F
Size	1	62.24	<1.0
Sex	1	92.56	<1.0
Size × sex	1	1061.76	5.55*
Error	30	197.44	

* $p < .05$.

clear. First there is no overall effect of room size. The groups in the small room made slightly more competitive choices than those in the large room (40.59 vs. 37.22) but this difference did not approach significance. Second, there was a strong size by sex interaction, with males being more competitive in the small than large room and with females showing a smaller and opposite pattern ($F = 5.55$, $p < .05$). Looked at separately the difference between large and small rooms for the males is significant ($F = 4.41$, $p < .05$) while the difference for females is not.

Appendix 5: Crowding and Aggressiveness and Emotional Reaction (In Collaboration with Stanley Heshka, Alan Levy, Roberta Welte Buchanan, and Judy Price) *

Method: There were 258 subjects ranging in age from eighteen to eighty, recruited through an ad in *The New York Times*. The sample was quite varied in terms of profession, economic level, and ethnic group. Participants were paid $8.00 for the four-hour experiment. In the first part of the study all-male and all-female groups ranging in size from six to ten were run. In the second part, mixed-sex groups of the same size were included.

The subjects were put in either large (about 300 square feet) or small (about 100 square feet) rooms for the duration of the study. The experiment was set up as a mock jury situation. The subjects listened to five taped condensations of courtroom cases and gave their verdict on each. The cases were created by us, but sounded quite realistic. They included cases of a hit-and-run accident, a purse-snatching in which an elderly lady was injured, arson in which somebody was burned, a man injured while burglarizing a car, and rape. All cases included witnesses for both sides, summations, and a judge's charge to the jury. They were designed to be somewhat ambiguous but to be weighted in favor of conviction. Subjects gave their verdicts without discussing the case, but for the last two cases they then held a discussion and gave another private verdict. For each case the subject indicated guilty or not guilty, and if guilty, how severe a sentence should be imposed.

For half of the groups a static-like white noise was played simultaneously with the last three cases. Subjects in all conditions were warned that the quality of the tapes was not good, but only those in the "noise" groups heard this unpleasant static. The purpose of this was to assess the effect of an irrele-

* This experiment is described fully in Freedman et al., 1972.

vant, additional irritation on the subjects' reaction to the situation.

After all of the cases had been heard and the verdicts given, all subjects answered a series of questions concerning their feelings about the experiment, the group, and the situation as a whole.

Table 5.1: Sentence Scores as a Function of Room Size and Sex

ROOM SIZE	ALL-MALE GROUPS	ALL-FEMALE GROUPS	MIXED-SEX GROUPS *Males Only*	MIXED-SEX GROUPS *Females Only*
Large	37.78	37.10	31.50	34.26
Small	38.87	32.95	31.11	35.25

Results: Severity of sentences. As shown in Table 5.1, the size of the room had no over-all effect on severity. There is a slight tendency for the larger rooms to be more severe, but this does not approach significance. In contrast, there is a strong sex-by-size interaction. The all-female groups were more lenient in the small than the large room while the males were somewhat more severe in the small room. ($F = 8.64$, $p < .05$.) The difference for females is significant ($F = 10.83$, $p < .05$) but for males it is not ($F < 1.0$). This pattern is consistent across noise and no-noise conditions. Indeed, adding the noise had no significant effects or interactions. It might be noted that the males are, in general, somewhat more severe than the females. The mixed-sex groups show no consistent pattern as a function of crowding—there are no overall effects of room size for the groups as a whole, nor are there any effects for males and females considered separately. The only appreciable effect is that the males in mixed-sex groups are much less severe than those in all-male groups—a result that is not relevant to our concern with crowding but may be of importance to lawyers and those interested in the effect of sexual segregation.

Affective reactions: The subjects' emotional responses to the situation are presented in Table 5.2. There are no overall effects of crowding or for noise, but there are substantial and consistent interactions of sex and crowding. On all questions involving positive or negative evaluations of the experience, females are more positive in the small than the large room while males show the opposite pattern. This held for how interesting the session was, how pleasant it was, how friendly

Table 5.2: Ratings of Group and Session as a Function of Sex and Room Size (on a Scale of 0–4)

	SMALL		LARGE		
	Male	*Female*	*Male*	*Female*	*F**
Interesting	1.87	2.29	1.88	1.91	1.98
Pleasant	1.85	2.33	1.98	1.68	4.54
Friendly	1.29	1.49	1.43	1.09	6.72
Like group	1.45	1.83	1.73	1.50	9.52
Better than average	1.32	1.62	1.40	1.45	3.00
Influenced	2.77	3.19	2.86	2.93	—

* *F* for sex-by-size interaction; $df = 1, 8$.
NOTE: The higher the number, the more positive the average rating by the group.

the group was, how much the subjects liked the other members of the group, and whether the group was a better than average jury. The first and last of these are the marginally significant, the other three are all significant. The final question (During the discussion was your opinion influenced by what the other members said?) did not involve affective reactions and did not show the typical pattern. Thus, the interaction seems to be quite specific to positive and negative feelings about the experience and the rest of the group. Once again, the mixed-sex groups showed no consistent interactions either for the group as a whole or for males and females considered separately.

Appendix 6: Crowding as an Intensifier of Pleasantness and Unpleasantness (In Collaboration with Stanley Heshka and Alan Levy)

Method. Subjects were high school students recruited by an ad in the *Palo Alto Times* and paid $6.00 for their time. There was a total of twenty groups of either all-female or mixed-sex subjects. The groups ranged in size from six to ten, and two groups were run at a time—one in a small room, one in a large room. The rooms used were about 70 and 150 square feet. The participants sat on the floor.

The situation was described as a study of public speaking and reactions to criticism. Each subject delivered a speech (which was provided for them) and the rest of the group gave suggestions on speaking techniques. The key element was that for half the groups these suggestions were all positive while for half they were all negative. In other words, in one condition, the subject was giving a speech and receiving only positive comments, and in the other the subject was receiving only negative comments. We assumed that this would cause the former condition to be pleasant and the latter unpleasant. After all participants had delivered their speeches, they filled out a questionnaire dealing with their reactions to the situation and the other members of the group.

Results: The subjects' responses to the questionnaire constitute the major source of data. There are no main effects of room size. The crowded and uncrowded subjects did not differ appreciably on any measure except a manipulation check on which those in the small room did, indeed, report that they were more crowded and that the room could hold fewer people. On no measure of attitude toward the other people or the session as a whole did the large and small rooms differ appreciably.

In contrast there is a consistent pattern of interactions of room size and pleasantness. The small room gave more positive ratings than the large room in the pleasant condition and more negative in the unpleasant condition. This interaction is

Table 6: Ratings of Group and Session as a Function of Density and Pleasantness

	PLEASANT CONDITION		UNPLEASANT CONDITION	
	Low Density	*High Density*	*Low Density*	*High Density*
Liked other people	2.01	2.22	2.10	1.92
Would participate again	2.38	2.74	2.48	2.21
Learning experience	2.01	2.30	1.70	1.48
Lively	1.26	1.65	1.65	1.22
Liked other speeches	4.50	4.61	3.79	3.63
Be with same people again	2.36	2.54	2.47	2.46

NOTE: On all scales a higher number is more positive.

significant for the ratings of the speech, how much the participants liked the other members of the group, and whether they would like to participate again. The pattern is the same for whether it was a good group, whether they would like to be with the same people if they participated again, and whether the discussion was lively. Although not all of these interactions reach acceptable levels of statistical significance, the pattern is consistent across many different questions and there are no appreciable reversals.

There was a consistent, though generally not significant tendency for the effects to be stronger for the all-female than for the mixed-sex groups. The direction of the interaction was usually the same for both kinds of groups, but was much clearer for all-females. This makes it appear that the effects of density as well as its interaction with other variables may depend to some extent on the sexual make-up of the groups.

Appendix 7: Crowding as an Intensifier of the Effect of Success and Failure (In Collaboration with Stanley Heshka and Alan Levy)

Method: The subjects were 133 male high school students recruited through an ad in the *Palo Alto Times* offering $5.00 for two hours' participation in a psychology experiment at Stanford University. Groups of six to eight subjects were put in either a large or small room (the same rooms used in the experiment described in Appendix 6).

The groups were given a series of fifteen problems that were presented one at a time at one-minute intervals. The task consisted of transforming one word into another by changing one letter at a time, being sure always that this produced an acceptable English word. For example, subjects were given the pair *gold—lead* and could solve the problem by the steps *gold—goad—load—lead.* The group worked as a team on each problem and were not allowed to spend more than the allotted one minute.

Half of the groups under each crowding condition were deliberately made to fail and half succeed on this series of problems. This was done by giving some groups eight difficult pairs which required four to six intermediate steps and seven easy pairs that required only two to four steps. The other group received all easy problems. All groups were told that an average performance was seven or eight correct, but groups that were given the easy list solved twelve or thirteen problems while those given the harder list solved only five to seven. Thus the success groups actually solved more problems and also thought they had done much better than average. The failure groups solved fewer than half and thought they had done worse than average.

After completing work on the fifteen problems, the participants filled out a questionnaire concerning their reactions to the group and the experience as a whole. They then worked on a second task, which was identical for all groups. It consisted of finding words that were hidden in an array of letters. Each subject received a different list, but was encouraged to give and get help from the rest of the group by passing the sheets around. The groups worked on this for fifteen minutes and then responded to a second questionnaire.

Results: The major dependent measures are the subjects' ratings of the other members of their group and the session as a whole, and their performance on the hidden-word task. On almost all of these the small-room groups were either more positive or there was an interaction of room size and success condition. The subjects in the small room liked each other more, were friendlier, and did better on the hidden-word task than those in the large room (all p's less than .05). The only exception to this pattern of main effects was the subjects' ratings of their own performance on the first task. Although they actually did somewhat better, those in the small room thought they had done worse and that the scores were more influenced by chance.

The pattern of interactions is similar to previous ones—the small room made the success condition more positive and the failure condition more negative. The small-room failure subjects were less willing to participate again with the same people than those in the large room, while the small-room success subjects were more willing than those in the large room. Similarly, the small-room failure subjects found the session more boring, less lively, and a worse experience in general than those in the large room, with this pattern reversed for the success groups. All of these interactions are significant (p's less than .05).

Appendix 8: Crowding, Aggressiveness, and External or Internal Crowding as an Intensifier of Internal vs. External Pleasantness (In Collaboration with Ilene Staff)

Method: The subjects were ninety-five persons connected with Columbia University (mostly students) who were paid $5.00 for their participation. They were run in mixed-sex groups of four to five people except for one all-female and one all-male group. They were put in either a small room (43 square feet) or a large room (102 square feet).

The procedure was similar to that of the experiment described in Appendix 6. Subjects gave talks and either all positive or all negative criticisms were made of their presentation.

The major difference from the earlier study was that this criticism was made either by the other members of the group (internal) or by a group that was observing through a two-way mirror (external). This internal-external manipulation was done within each group by using written instructions. Half of each group thought the group itself was writing criticisms, half thought only the outside group was. In order to make this plausible, the external subjects were told that they and the rest of the group would be counting the number of times a particular common word or class of words was used in the speech, while the internal subjects were told that this was being done by the observers. Thus, for all subjects, the members of the group had a task and would be writing, but the nature of the task involved either criticisms or neutral counting of words. After all participants had given talks, they filled out a questionnaire designed to assess their mood and reactions to the experience.

Results. The internal condition was a replication of other work. There was some tendency for the crowded groups to respond more positively than the uncrowded. Those in the small room liked the group more ($F = 7, 43$, $\rho < .05$), were less anxious during the speech ($F = 16, 17$, $p < .01$), and enjoyed the experiment more ($F = 2.56$, $p < .17$). No other differences were appreciable in either direction.

The typical interactions between crowding and pleasantness appeared even more strongly than in previous studies. The small-room positive subjects liked their group more than the large-room positive subjects, while the small-room negative subjects liked the rest of the group less than the large-room negative subjects ($F = 8.31$, $p < .05$). Similar interactions occurred for ratings of overall mood, willingness to participate again, and quality of the day. Less strong interactions in the pattern held for almost all relevant questions. The only exceptions were ratings of anxiety and enjoyment of the session (which had no appreciable interactions).

When all conditions are combined, most of these interactions hold. Within just the external condition, however, the effects are much weaker and most effects disappear entirely. There is still a significant effect on boringness of the session ($F = 5.63$, $p < .05$) and a slight effect on enjoyment ($F = 3.06$, $p < .15$). All other interactions either disappear or are in the opposite direction, though none approach significance. Thus, when the pleasantness of the experience is due to an external factor, the density does not seem to intensify reactions.

NOTES

Chapter 1: What Is Crowding?

PAGE 4 Some authors have assumed that crowding means stress and have defined it accordingly, e.g., Desor (1972), Ittleson *et al.* (1970), Stokols (1972). This obviously takes as conclusion what is at issue—how crowding affects people. We are not asking whether crowding is stressful, helpful, or anything else, so we must not assume that it is any of these. Stokols did make the important distinction between physical and psychological crowding, the former referring to the amount of space and the latter to the internal feeling. But he then seems to emphasize the latter, whereas it is mainly the former that must be studied.

Chapter 2: Colonies, Swarms, and Herds

PAGE 12 Work on lemmings by Clough (1965, 1968).

PAGE 13 Research on deer by Christian, Flyger, and Davis (1960).

PAGE 15 Observations of enclosed animals in laboratories: Calhoun (1962), Christian (1965), Snyder (1968), Southwick (1955). There are many other similar studies cited in the Bibliography.

PAGE 20 Adrenal effects: Christian, Flyger, and Davis (1960), Christian (1955), Brain and Nowell (1971), Morrison and Thatcher (1969), Siegel (1959), and many others have found enlarged adrenals in group-reared animals or those who were subjected to crowding in their natural environment. However, some studies, e.g., Southwick and Bland (1959), McKeever (1959), Thiessen (1964), found either no effects or very small ones. Despite the lack of perfect consistency, it does seem that being in a group results in higher adrenal activity than being alone. There is considerable question that larger groups produce stronger effects than smaller ones.

PAGE 20 Gonadal effects: Christian (1955), Thiessen (1964), Southwick and Bland (1959), and Snyder (1968) all studied this problem and each study found some evidence of decreased gonadal function. However, the findings were inconsistent—some getting results on one measure, some on another. And none of the investigators report any actual pathology of testes or vesicles.

PAGE 21 Disease effects: Plaut *et al.* (1969) found that grouped mice were less resistant, although the size of the cage (and thus the density) was unimportant. The same group of investigators (Friedman *et al.* [1970]) later found that grouped animals were more resistant to another disease. Ader (1965) and Conger, Sawrey, and Turrell (1958) report no differences between grouped and individual animals in susceptibility to ulcers.

PAGE 22 Emotionality: Morrison and Thatcher (1969), Ader *et al.* (1963), Thiessen (1964), and Thiessen, Zolman, and Rodgers (1962) all found that grouped animals were, if anything, less emotional than individually raised animals.

Chapter 3: Animal Theories

PAGE 24 Territoriality: Ardrey (1966) is a popularized account of this idea. It is also discussed in Lorenz (1966).

PAGE 24 Tropical fish quotation: Lorenz (1966), p. 8.

PAGE 26 Wolves: Mowat (1963).

PAGE 27 Territoriality and food supply: Kluyver and Tinbergen (1953), Pitelka *et al.* (1955). This evidence is at best suggestive.

PAGE 30 Rabbit study: Myers *et al.* (1971).

PAGE 32 Homeostatic theories: Wynne-Edwards (1965), Christian (1950), Christian, Lloyd, and Davis (1965).

PAGE 37 Nesting spaces: although Calhoun provides "apartment houses" with special nesting spaces, there is still a shortage of good apartments. The dominant males often prevent access to many areas even if they are not using them, thus further reducing available spaces. A good administrator might be able to divide up the space so that all animals had a good spot, but in reality there is a severe shortage.

Chapter 4: From Mice to Men?

PAGE 41 Ethologists who generalize their findings to people: Lorenz (1966), Morris (1967), Ardrey (1966), Tiger (1969). There is always some temptation to make statements about humans based on how animals behave, but these authors have yielded so much to this temptation that their statements are made as if they had scientific research to support them. It is one thing to get clues and hints about human behavior from observing animals; it is quite a different matter to assert truths about humans from a knowledge of nonhumans. On the other hand, it is also important to distinguish between eminent ethologists such as Lorenz, who is a Nobel Prize winner and one of the most important and productive men in the field, and popularizers such as Morris and Ardrey. Although it is a mistake for anyone to generalize findings further than is warranted, coming from outstanding scientists such as Lorenz and Tinbergen these ideas carry at least the weight of their great experience and knowledge. And, in fact, even when making statements with which I would disagree, Lorenz tends to treat them as opinions based on his observations rather than as scientific facts.

PAGE 42 Darwinian approach: it should be clear that this viewpoint is extremely important in understanding much about biological development. If it were more widely applied, it would probably be helpful to psychologists and other social scientists, who too rarely look for the utility of a pattern of behavior or an institution. The only complaint is with those who go further than the theory warrants and make the Panglossian assumption that every animal is a perfect creature in a perfect world.

PAGE 45 Desmond Morris—all references are to the Corgi Book edition, 1968, reprint.

PAGE 45 Morris quote from page 9.

PAGE 45 Nocturnal prowl for domestic cats—Morris, page 23.

PAGE 46 Man's stamina—Morris, page 29.

PAGE 47 Sexual behavior of all men based on White North Americans—Morris, pages 45–46.

PAGE 48 Divorce rate of 0.9 per cent (bond breaking up)—Morris, page 55. Since this seemed so unlikely, it was checked in other editions and appears in them also. It is conceivable that Morris is referring to the number of divorces compared to the total population of the country or the total existing marriages. If so, it is a meaningless figure, since what matters is the percentage of marriages that do not last, not the percentage that break up in any given year. In the United States a very high percentage of marriages end in divorce—the rate varying from 25 per cent to more than 50 per cent from state to state. Clearly, many pair bonds, even those institutionalized in legal marriage, do not last. And, of course, vast numbers of nonlegal pair bonds—affairs, people living together, and so on—end with separation.

PAGE 49 Contraception and promiscuity—Morris, page 88.

PAGE 49 Hymen preventing sexual intercourse—Morris, page 73.

PAGE 50 Territoriality, 1966—Ardrey, page 95.

PAGE 50 Farming in U.S. and Russia as evidence for territoriality—Ardrey, pages 105ff.

Chapter 5: Crowding and Crime

PAGE 56 These data are drawn from the report of the National Commission on the Causes and Prevention of Violence that was published in 1970.

PAGE 58 Population density and pathology. More and more of these studies are being conducted and the results continue to support the contention that density is unrelated to crime or other negative effects. Some of these studies are: metropolitan areas—Pressman and Carol (1971); cities—Galle *et al.* (1972). These authors include total population as part of their measure of density and accordingly confuse two entirely different factors. Their index of density must therefore be disregarded. To be fair to them, however, they do reach a modest conclusion that their findings are consistent with the idea that density has negative effects, not that this has been proved. We do not agree with even this modest statement, but the authors have been cautious.

PAGE 60 Galle *et al.* (1972). Again Galle *et al.* interpret their data as showing a negative effect, or at least being consistent with this interpretation, while we would draw the opposite conclusions.

To be mentioned again later, Mitchell (1971), in Hong Kong, and Booth and Cowell (1974), in Canada, have done massive studies interviewing individuals who live under high-

and low-density conditions. Both of these impressive studies found no appreciable effects of density on health.

PAGE 65 Jane Jacobs (1962).

PAGE 68 Mitchell (1971), Booth and Cowell (1974). There are also a number of unpublished papers by Booth and his associates presenting the results of a long-term study of this problem in Canada. In all of this work, the effects of density are reported to be small, inconsistent, and clearly not generally negative.

PAGE 68 Lest it be thought that my colleagues and I are alone in our belief that crowding is not harmful, let me note that many other authors in the field are now coming to similar conclusions. We have all been reluctant to accept it, but the research has become more and more convincing. For example, Gad (1973) summarizes the available evidence and concludes that the results do not support the idea that crowding produces negative effects on people. And in concluding a series of papers on this topic, Booth agrees that there have been no consistent demonstrations of negative effects of high density. It is always difficult to prove that something does not exist—if you see it, you believe it is there; if you do not see it, there is still the chance that it is there but you have missed it. But there is a large and growing body of literature indicating that density does not have generally bad effects on people, and more and more researchers in the field are accepting this.

Chapter 6: Personal Space and Isolation

PAGE 71 Personal space: Hall (1959, 1966, etc.), Sommer (1969), and many others.

PAGE 71 Preferred distances for friends versus acquaintances and for different ethnic groups: Hall (1966), Watson and Graves (1966), Aiello and Cooper (1972), Gottheil, Corey, and Parades (1968), Guardo and Meisels (1971), to cite a few of the many references to support these consistent effects.

PAGE 73 Library study: Felipe and Sommer (1966).

PAGE 74 Isolation studies: Altman and Haythorn (1965, 1967), Altman, Taylor, and Wheeler (1971), Smith and Haythorn (1972). It should be noted that in some of these studies, some of the groups fail to complete the scheduled stay in isolation. There is little evidence of breakdown or any severe reactions, but the groups simply refuse to remain any longer. Nevertheless, in most studies all or most of the groups stay in isolation as long as the experimenters ask them to.

PAGE 75 Privacy and more space versus no privacy and less space: Taylor, Wheeler, and Altman (1968).

PAGE 75 Small rooms versus large rooms, with less hostility in the former: Smith and Haythorn (1972).

Chapter 7: Crowding, Aggression, and Sex

PAGE 77 Ehrlich, *The Population Bomb* (1968).

PAGE 81 Task performance: Griffitt and Veitch (1971).

PAGE 83 Observational studies of crowding: Hutt and Vaizey (1966), McGrew (1970), and Price (1971).

PAGE 87 Experimental studies showing sex differences in response to crowding: Ross *et al.* (1973), Marshall and Heslin (unpublished), Loo (1972). In addition, there are quite a few very recent articles, still unpublished, that have produced the same kind of patterns. Males and females react differently to high density under a wide variety of conditions. However, the specific differences are not consistent and seem to depend on the exact circumstances. There is no evidence from this work that either sex is more sensitive to density, or that one always responds more negatively or more positively than the other.

Chapter 10: Density and Design

PAGE 120 We should note that many, if not all, of the ideas suggested have been proposed by others. The point is that the work on the effect of density provides a scientific foundation for suggestions that have previously been based primarily on intuition and personal experience. Those who have at times argued against these kinds of proposals have often used the supposed negative effects of high density as ammunition. Since we now believe that high density does not have negative effects, ideas for housing and other urban problems must be consistent with and make use of this knowledge. In particular, it is no longer possible to argue against high-density housing because it is necessarily harmful.

PAGE 122 Anonymity: research indicates that people who are anonymous are more likely to engage in antisocial behavior. Singer, Brush, and Lublin (1965), Zimbardo (1969), and others. Although there is no controlled research, it also seems likely that anonymity reduces pro-social behavior, such as offering help and contributing to charity.

PAGE 122 Bystanders not helping when they are in large groups: a great deal of research has shown that offering help in emergencies is less likely to occur when people are in groups than when they are alone. This is particularly true if all the people involved are strangers and if it appears that someone else may help. Darley and Latané (1968), Latané and Darley (1968), Smith, Smythe, and Lien (1972), and many others.

PAGE 123 Proximity and friendship: the closer people live, the more likely they are to become friends. This applies to people who live in adjacent houses, and also to people living on the same floor of an apartment house. Festinger, Schachter, and Back (1950), Whyte (1956).

PAGE 127 The effects of density in Hong Kong: Mitchell (1971).

PAGE 128 Positive view of high-density housing: Whyte (1968).

BIBLIOGRAPHY

ADER, R. "The Influence of Psychological Factors on Disease Susceptibility in Animals." In Conalty, M. L., ed., *Husbandry of Laboratory Animals.* New York: Academic Press (1967), pp. 219–38.

———. "Effects of Early Experience and Differential Housing on Behavior and Susceptibility to Gastric Erosions in the Rat." *Journal of Comparative and Physiological Psychology* (1965), 60:233.

ADER, R., KREUTNER, A., JR., and JACOBS, H. L. "Social Environment, Emotionality and Alloxan Diabetes in the Rat." *Psychosomatic Medicine* (1963), 25:60.

AIELLO, J. R., and COOPER, R. E. "The Use of Personal Space as a Function of Social Affect." *Proceedings of the 80th Annual Convention of the American Psychology Association* (1972), 7:207–08.

ALBERT, S., and DABBS, J. M., JR. "Physical Distance and Persuasion." *Journal of Personality and Social Psychology* (1970), 15:265–70.

ALBERT, Z. "The Effect of Number of Animals per Cage on the Development of Spontaneous Neoplasms." In Conalty, M. L., ed., *Husbandry of Laboratory Animals.* New York: Academic Press (1967), pp. 275–84.

ALTMAN, I., and HAYTHORN, W. W. "The Effects of Social Isolation and Group Composition on Performance." *Human Relations* (1967b), 4:313–40.

———. "Interpersonal Exchange in Isolation." *Sociometry* (1965), 28:411–26.

ALTMAN, I., TAYLOR, D. A., and WHEELER, L. "Ecological Aspects of Group Behavior in Social Isolation." *Journal of Applied Social Psychology* (1971), 1:76–100.

ARDREY, R. *The Territorial Imperative.* New York: Atheneum, 1966.

ARGYLE, M., and DEAN, J. "Eye Contact, Distance and Affiliation." *Sociometry* (1965), 28:289–304.

BOOTH, A., and COWELL, J. "The Effects of Crowding upon Health." Paper presented at the American Population Association Meetings, New York, 1974.

BRAIN, P. F., and NOWELL, N. W. "Isolation versus Grouping Effects on Adrenal and Gonadal Functions in Albino Mice. 1. The Male." *General Comparative Endocrinology* (1971), 16:149–54.

BRONSON, F. H. "Effects of Social Stimulation on Adrenal and Reproductive Physiology of Rodents." In Conalty, M. L., ed., *Husbandry of Laboratory Animals.* New York: Academic Press, 1967.

CALHOUN, J. B. "Phenomena Associated with Population Density." *Proceedings of the National Academy of Sciences* (1961), 47:428–49.

———. "Population Density and Social Pathology." *Scientific American* (1962), 206:139–48.

———. "A 'Behavioral Sink.' " In Bliss, E. L., ed., *Roots of Behavior.* New York: Harper, 1962.

CARSON, D. "Population Concentration and Human Stress." In B. F. Rourke, ed., *Explorations in the Psychology of Stress and Anxiety.* Ontario: Longmans Canada Limited (1969), pp. 27–41.

CASSEL, J. "Health Consequences of Population Density and Crowding." In R. Gutman, ed., *People and Buildings.* New York: Basic Books (1972), p. 251.

CHITTY, D., "The Natural Selection of Self-Regulatory Behavior in Animal Populations." *Proceedings of the Ecological Society of Australia* (1967), 2:51–78.

CHITTY, D. "Variations in the Weight of the Adrenal Glands of the Field Vole (*Microtus agrestis*)." *Journal of Endocrinology* (1961), 22:387–93.

CHRISTIAN, J. J. "The Adreno-Pituitary System and Population Cycles in Mammals." *Journal of Mammalogy* (1950), 31:247–59.

———. "Effect of Population Size on the Adrenal Glands and Reproductive Organs of Male White Mice." *American Journal of Physiology* (1955), 181:477–80.

———. "The Role of Endocrine and Behavioral Factors in the Growth of Mammalian Populations." In Gorbman, ed.,

Comparative Endocrinology. New York: Wiley (1959), 71–97.

———. "Endocrine Adaptive Mechanisms and the Physiologic Regulation of Population Growth." In Mayer and Van Gelder, eds., *Physiological Mammalogy*. New York: Academic Press (1963), pp. 189–353.

CHRISTIAN, J. J., FLYGER, V., and DAVIS, D. C. "Factors in the Mass Mortality of a Herd of Sika Deer, *Cervus nippon*." *Chesapeake Science* (1960), 1:79–95.

CHRISTIAN, J. J., LLOYD, J. A., and DAVIS, D. E. "The Role of Endocrines in the Self-Regulation of Mammalian Populations." *Recent Progress in Hormone Research* (1965), 21:501–78.

CLOUGH, G. C. "Lemmings and Population Problems." *American Scientist* (1965), 53:99–212.

———. "Social Behavior and Ecology of Norwegian Lemmings during a Population Peak and Crash." Papers of the Norwegian state game research institute (1968), 2:328.

CONGER, J. J., SAWREY, W. L., and TURRELL, E. S. "The Role of Social Experience in the Production of Gastric Ulcers in Hooded Rats Placed in a Conflict Situation." *Journal of Abnormal and Social Psychology* (1958), 57:214.

DARLEY, J. M., and LATANÉ, B. "Bystander Intervention in Emergencies: Diffusion of Responsibility." *Journal of Personality and Social Psychology* (1968), 8:377–83.

DAVIS, D. E. "Physiological Effects of Continued Crowding." In A. Esser, ed., *Behavior and Environment*. New York: Plenum Press (1971), p. 143.

DESOR, J. A. "Toward a Psychological Theory of Crowding." *Journal of Personality and Social Psychology* (1972), 21:79–83.

DUBOS, R. "The Social Environment." In H. M. Proshansky, W. H. Ittelson, and L. G. Rivlin, eds., *Environmental Psychology*. New York: Holt, Rinehart & Winston (1970), pp.202–08.

EHRLICH, P. R. *The Population Bomb*. New York: Ballantine, 1968.

ELLSWORTH, P. C., CARLSMITH, J. M., and HENSON, A. "The Stare as a Stimulus to Flight in Human Subjects: A Series of Field Experiments." *Journal of Personality and Social Psychology* (1972), 21:302–11.

ESSER, A. *Behavior and Environment: The Use of Space by Animals and Men*. New York: Plenum Press, 1971.

———. "Experiences of Crowding: Illustration of a Paradigm

for Man-Environment Relations." *Representative Research in Social Psychology* (1973), 4, 207–18.

FELIPE, N., and SOMMER, R. "Invasions of Personal Space." *Social Problems* (1966), 14:206–14.

FESTINGER, L., SCHACHTER, S., and BACK, K. *Social Pressures in Informal Groups: A Study of Human Factors in Housing.* New York: Harper and Row (1950), chapter 3.

FREEDMAN, J., KLEVANSKY, S., and EHRLICH, P. "The Effect of Crowding on Human Task Performance." *Journal of Applied Social Psychology* (1971), 1:7–25.

FREEDMAN, J., LEVY, A., BUCHANAN, R. W., and PRICE, J. "Crowding and Human Aggressiveness." *Journal of Experimental Social Psychology* (1972), 8:528–48.

FREEDMAN, J. L. "Conceptualization of Crowding." Paper prepared for the Commission on Population Growth and the American Future, 1972.

FREEDMAN, J. L., HESHKA, S., and LEVY, A. "Population Density and Crime in Metropolitan U. S. Areas." Unpublished, 1973.

———. "Population Density and Pathology: Is There a Relationship?" *Journal of Experimental Social Psychology*, in press, 1974.

FRIEDMAN, S. B., GLASGOW, L. A., and ADER, R. "Psychosocial Factors Modifying Host Resistance to Experimental Infections." *Annals of the New York Academy of Sciences* (1969), 164:381.

FRIEDMAN, S. B., LOWELL, A. G., and ADER, R. "Differential Susceptibility to a Viral Agent in Mice Housed Alone or in Groups." *Psychosomatic Medicine* (1970), 32:285–99.

GALLE, O. R., GOVE, W. R., and MC PHERSON, J. M. "Population Density and Pathology: What Are the Relations for Man." *Science* (1972), 176:23–30.

GALLE, O. R., MC CARTHY, J. D., and GOVE, W. "Population Density and Pathology." Paper presented at the Annual Meeting of the Population Association of America, New York, 1974.

GLASS, D., and SINGER, J. *Urban Stress.* New York: Academic Press, 1972.

GRIFFITT, W., and VEITCH, R. "Hot and Crowded: Influences of Population Density and Temperature on Interpersonal Affective Behavior." *Journal of Personality and Social Psychology* (1971), 17:92–98.

GOTTHEIL, E., COREY, J., and PARADES, A. "Psychological and

Physical Dimensions of Personal Space." *Journal of Psychology* (1968), 69:7–9.

GUARDO, C. J., and MEISELS, M. "Child-Parent Spatial Patterns under Praise and Reproof." *Developmental Psychology* (1971), 5:365.

HALL, E. T. *The Silent Language*. Garden City, N.Y.: Doubleday, 1959.

———. "A System for the Notation of Proxemic Behavior." *American Anthropologist* (1963), 65:1003–27.

———. *The Hidden Dimension*. Garden City, N.Y.: Doubleday, 1966.

HAYTHORN, W. W., ALTMAN, I., and MYERS, T. I. "Emotional Symptomatology and Stress in Isolated Pairs of Men." *Journal of Experimental Research in Personality* (1966), 4:290–306.

HUTT, C., and VAIZEY, M. J. "Differential Effects of Group Density on Social Behavior." *Nature* (1966), 209:1371–72.

ITTELSON, W. H., PROSHANSKY, H. M., and RIVLIN, L. G. "The Environmental Psychology of the Psychiatric Ward." In H. M. Proshansky, W. H. Ittelson, and L. G. Rivlin, eds., *Environmental Psychology*. New York: Holt, Rinehart & Winston, 1970.

JACOBS, J. *Death and Life of Great American Cities*. New York: Random House, 1961.

———. *The Economy of Cities*. New York: Random House, 1969, p. 161.

KLUYVER, H. N., and TINBERGEN, L. "Territory and the Regulation of Density in Titmice." *Archives néerlandaises de zoologie* (1953), 10:265–89.

LATANÉ, B., and DARLEY, J. M. "Group Inhibition of Bystander Intervention in Emergencies," *Journal of Personality and Social Psychology* (1968), 10:215–21.

LE BON, G. *The Crowd*, New York: The Viking Press, 1960 (Orig., 1895).

LIEBMAN, M. "The Effects of Sex and Race Norms on Personal Space." *Environment and Behavior* (1970), 2:208–46.

LOO, C. M. "The Effects of Spatial Density on the Social Behavior of Children." *Journal of Applied Social Psychology* (1972), 2:372–81.

LORENZ, K. S. *On Aggression*. New York: Harcourt Brace Jovanovich, 1966.

LOUCH, C. D. "Adrenocortical Activity in Relation to the Density and Dynamics of Three Confined Populations of *Microtus pennsylvanicus*." *Ecology* (1956), 37:701–13.

MARSHALL, J. E., and HESLIN, R. "Boys and Girls Together: Sexual Group Composition and the Effect of Density and Group Size on Cohesiveness." Unpublished, 1974.

MC GREW, P. "Social and Spacing Density Effects on Spacing Density in Preschool Children." *Journal of Child Psychology and Psychiatry* (1970), 11:197–205.

MC GREW, W. C. "An Ethological Study of Social Behavior in Preschool Children." Unpublished doctoral dissertation. Oxford University, 1970.

MC KEEVER, S. "Effects of Reproductive Activity on the Weight of Adrenal Glands in *Mocrotus montanus*." *The Anatomical Record* (1959), 135:1–5.

MITCHELL, R. E. "Some Social Implications of High-Density Housing." *American Sociological Review* (1971), 36:18–29.

MORRIS, D. *The Naked Ape.* London: Jonathan Cape, 1967. (References in text are to Corgi edition, 1968.)

MORRISON, B. J., and THATCHER, K. "Overpopulation Effects on Social Reduction of Emotionality in the Albino Rat." *Journal of Comparative and Physiological Psychology* (1969), 69:658–62.

MOWAT, F. *Never Cry Wolf.* New York: Laurel, 1963.

MUNROE, R. L., and MUNROE, R. H. "Population Density and Affective Relationships in Three East African Societies." *Journal of Social Psychology* (1972), 88:15–18.

MYERS, K. "The Effects of Density on Sociality and Health in Mammals." *Proceedings of the Ecological Society of Australia* (1966), 1:40–64.

MYERS, K., HALE, C. S., MYKYTOWYCZ, and HUGHES, R. L. "The Effects of Varying Density and Space on Sociality and Health in Animals." In A. Esser, ed., *Behavior and Environment.* New York: Plenum Press, 1971.

The National Commission on the Causes and Prevention of Violence. *To Establish Justice, to Insure Domestic Tranquility.* New York: Praeger, 1970.

PITELKA, F. A., TOMICH, P. Q., and TREICHEL, G. W. "Ecological Relations of Jaegers and Owls as Lemming Predators Near Barrow, Alaska." *Ecological Monographs* (1955), 25:85–117.

PLAUT, S. M., ADER, R., FRIEDMAN, S. B., and RITTERSON, A. L. "Social Factors in Resistance to Malaria in the Mouse: Effects of Groups vs. Individual Housing on Resistance to *Plasmodium berghei* Infection." *Psychosomatic Medicine* (1969), 31:536–52.

PRESSMAN, I., and CAROL, A. "Crime as a Diseconomy of Scale." *Review of Social Economy* (1971), 29:227–36.

PRICE, J. "The Effects of Crowding on the Social Behavior of Children." Unpublished doctoral dissertation. Columbia University, 1971.

RODGERS, D. A., and THIESSEN, D. D. "Effects of Population Density on Adrenal Size, Behavioral Arousal, and Alcohol Preferences of Inbred Mice." *Quarterly Journal of Studies on Alcohol* (1964), 25:240–47.

ROSS, M., LAYTON, B., ERICKSON, B., and SCHOPLER, J. "Affect, Facial Regard and Reactions to Crowding." *Journal of Personality and Social Psychology* (1973), 28:68–76.

SCHMITT, R. C. "Density, Health, and Social Disorganization." *Journal of American Institute of Planners* (1966), 32:38–40.

———. "Density, Delinquency and Crime in Honolulu." *Sociology and Social Research* (1957), 41:274–76.

SHERROD, D. "Crowding, Perceived Control and Behavioral After-Effects." Unpublished manuscript. Kirkland College, 1973.

SIEGEL, H. S. "Effect of Population Density on the Pituitary-Adrenal Cortical Axis of Cockerels." *Poultry Science* (1960), 39:500–10.

———. "Egg Production Characteristics and Adrenal Function in White Leghorns Confined at Different Floor-Space Levels." *Poultry Science* (1959), 38:893–98.

———. "The Relation between Crowding and Weight of Adrenal Glands in Chickens." *Ecology* (1959), 40:494–98.

SINGER, J. E., BRUSH, A., and LUBLIN, D. "Some Aspects of Deindividuation: Identification and Conformity." *Journal of Experimental Social Psychology* (1965), 1:356–78.

SMITH, S., AND HAYTHORN, W. H. "Effects of Compatibility, Crowding, Group Size, and Leadership Seniority on Stress, Anxiety, Hostility, and Annoyance in Isolated Groups." *Journal of Personality and Social Psychology* (1972), 22:67–79.

SMITH, R. E., SMYTHE, L., and LIEN, D. "Inhibition of Helping Behavior by a Similar or Dissimilar Nonreactive Fellow Bystander." *Journal of Personality and Social Psychology* (1972), 23:414–19.

SNYDER, R. L. "Reproduction and Population Pressures." In E. Stellar and J. M. Sprague, eds., *Progress in Physiological Psychology*. New York: Academic Press, 1968, pp. 119–60.

SOMMER, R. "The Distance for Comfortable Conversation: A Further Study." *Sociometry* (1962), 25:111–16.

———. "Studies in Personal Space." *Sociometry* (1959), 22:247–60.

———. *Personal Space: The Behavioral Basis of Design*. Englewood Cliffs, N.J.: Prentice-Hall, 1969.

SOUTHWICK, C. H. "The Population Dynamics of Confined House Mice Supplied with Unlimited Food." *Ecology* (1955), 36:212–25.

———. "Regulatory Mechanisms in House Mouse Populations: Social Behavior Affecting Litter Survival." *Ecology* (1955), 36:627–34.

———. "An Experimental Study of Intragroup Agonistic Behavior in Rhesus Monkeys (*Macaca mulatta*)." *Behavior* (1967), 28:182–209.

SOUTHWICK, C. H., and BLAND, V. P. "Effect of Population Density on Adrenal Glands and Reproductive Organs of CFW Mice." *American Journal of Physiology* (1959), 197:111–14.

STOKOLS, D. "On the Distinction between Density and Crowding: Some Implications for Future Research." *Psychological Review* (1972), 79:275–77.

———. "A Social Psychological Model of Crowding Phenomena." *Journal of the American Institute of Planners* (1972), 38:72–84.

STOKOLS, D., RALL, M., PINNER, B., and SCHOPLER, J. "Physical, Social and Personal Determinants of the Perception of Crowding." *Environment and Behavior* (1973), 5:87–115.

TAYLOR, D. A., WHEELER, L., and ALTMAN, I. "Stress Relations in Socially Isolated Groups." *Journal of Personality and Social Psychology* (1968), 9:369–76.

THIESSEN, D. D. "Population Density, Mouse Genotype, and Endocrine Function in Behavior." *Journal of Comparative and Physiological Psychology* (1964), 57:412–16.

THIESSEN, D. D., and RODGERS, D. A. "Population Density and Endocrine Function." *Psychological Bulletin* (1961), 58:441–51.

THIESSEN, D. D., ZOLMAN, J. F., and RODGERS, D. A. "Relation between Adrenal Weight, Brain Cholinesterase Activity, and Hole-in-Wall Behavior of Mice under Different Living Conditions." *Journal of Comparative Physiological Psychology* (1962), 55:186–90.

TIGER, L. *Men in Groups.* New York: Random House, 1969.

TOBACH, E., and BLOCH, H. "Effects of Stress by Crowding Prior to and Following Tuberculosis Infection." *American Journal of Physiology* (1956), 187:399–407.

WARD, S. K. "Overcrowding and Social Pathology: A Reexamination of the Implications for the Human Population." Paper presented at the Annual Meeting of the Population Association of America, New York, 1974.

WATSON, O. M, and GRAVES, T. "Quantitative Research in Proxemic Behavior." *American Anthropologist* (1966), 68:971–85.

WHYTE, WILLIAM., H., JR. *The Last Landscape.* New York: Doubleday, 1968.

WINSBOROUGH, H. H. "The Social Consequences of High Population Density." *Law and Contemporary Problems* (1965), 30:120–26.

WYNNE-EDWARDS, V. C. "Self-Regulating Systems in Populations of Animals." *Science* (1965), 147:1543–48.

ZAJONC, R. B "Social Facilitation." *Science* (1965), 149:269–74.

ZIMBARDO, P. G. "The Human Choice: Individuation, Reason, and Order versus Deindividuation, Impulse and Chaos." In W. J. Arnold and D. Levine, eds., *Nebraska Symposium on Motivation, 1969.* Lincoln: University of Nebraska Press, 1970, pp. 237–307.

ZLUTNICK, S., and ALTMAN, I. "Crowding and Human Behavior." In J. F. Wolhlwill and S. H. Carson, eds. *Environment and the Social Sciences; Perspectives and Applications.* Washington, D.C.: American Psychological Association, 1972.

INDEX